Thank you for picking up my book. Your support means a lot, and I hope you find the read both enjoyable and insightful. Beyond being an author, my work extends into research and consultancy within organizational behavior and leadership. I engage with a broad spectrum of clients, from individuals to larger teams and organizations, offering guidance in leadership development.

For a deeper dive into my professional background and consulting philosophy, several websites are available. There, you'll also find my contact details. I'm eager to hear your thoughts on the book or discuss potential collaboration in leadership coaching.

Discover more about my work and other publications related to leadership and organizational behavior at my personal website, https://thomaspatrickhuber.com.

Learn about my specific approach to leadership coaching and consulting at https://elevateus.ch, the official website of my company.

Lastly, in case you want to reach out to me directly please send me an email at thomaspatrick@mac.com.

I appreciate your support in purchasing this book and look forward to connecting with you.

Wishing you an enlightening journey,

Thomas P Huber, PhD, MS ECS

Dedication

To all the leaders who find the courage to lead with intention, with heart, and above all, with purpose,

To those who rise with the dawn, fueled not just by ambition but by a deep-seated desire to improve the lives of others,

For the executives who make tough choices, always guided by a moral compass that points to a destination greater than profit alone,

To the managers who understand that leadership is not just about delegating tasks, but about empowering individuals to reach their full potential,

For the mentors who invest time in nurturing the next generation, fully aware that their legacy will be judged not by numbers, but by the lives they've touched,

And for the unsung heroes, who may not bear the title of leader but influence their surroundings with integrity and purpose,

To the brave souls who dare to challenge the status quo, who risk ridicule and failure in the pursuit of something far more significant,

This book is lovingly and respectfully dedicated to you.

May your journey of purposeful leadership serve as a beacon for others to follow. May you remain steadfast in the face of challenges, inspired in the quest for innovation, and anchored by the profound impact you can make.

Your leadership does not just move people—it moves the world.

Introduction: Why Leading with Purpose is More Critical Than Ever

In an era marked by rapid technological advancements, increasing complexity, and unyielding competition, it's easy to lose sight of what truly matters. Leaders may find themselves navigating a landscape filled with metrics, KPIs, and deadlines, all while trying to keep a team motivated and focused. But there's an ingredient often missing in this recipe for success: Purpose.

Purpose is not just a feel-good buzzword or a motivational poster on the wall; it's the underlying force that drives not only individuals but entire organizations toward meaningful goals. It serves as the North Star, guiding us when the road ahead is murky. It pushes us to persevere in the face of challenges and propels us toward genuine impact. In essence, leading with purpose is about aligning our daily actions and decisions with a larger vision that extends beyond ourselves.

This book aims to explore the intricate yet compelling concept of purposeful leadership, break down its components, and offer actionable insights to integrate it into your own leadership style. We'll journey together through the historical background, delve into real-world case studies, and unlock the tools necessary for enacting change. This book also includes expert opinions and interviews to provide a well-rounded perspective on how purpose can redefine leadership paradigms.

Whether you are a seasoned executive, an aspiring leader, or someone looking to infuse more meaning into your work, this book is designed to equip you with the knowledge and tools to lead with purpose. Prepare to challenge your preconceptions, inspire your team, and achieve objectives you previously thought unattainable.

Because leadership is not just about hitting targets—it's about aiming for something far greater.

Purposeful leadership involves a conscious commitment to guide your actions and decisions through a lens of meaningful objectives. It transcends traditional notions of leadership that focus solely on profit, control, or authority. Leading with purpose is about adding a layer of intentionality to your role, one that extends its impact beyond your immediate surroundings to contribute positively to the community, society, or even the world at large.

In today's rapidly evolving landscape, characterized by environmental challenges, social disparities, and political complexities, leading with mere efficiency is insufficient. Leadership needs a moral and ethical framework; it needs purpose. In a world hungry for authentic leaders, the need for purpose-driven leadership is more pressing than ever. It serves as the glue that holds organizations together in times of crisis and the catalyst that drives innovation and progress.

As you turn the pages of this book, you'll find various tools and techniques to identify, articulate, and implement your purpose. You'll learn how to align your team's efforts with broader objectives for higher motivation and satisfaction. We will analyze compelling case studies that demonstrate the transformative power of leading with purpose. Through a blend of expert insights and practical advice, you'll come to see how purpose can be the driving force behind effective leadership.

By the end of this book, you'll have a richer understanding of what it means to lead with purpose and how to apply this approach in your own leadership journey. We aim to arm you with the knowledge and confidence you need to not just be a leader, but a leader who brings a deep sense of purpose to the table.

Part I: Understanding Purpose

Before diving into the mechanics of how to lead with purpose, it's crucial to establish a solid understanding of what "purpose" really means. This part of the book serves as a foundational exploration of that very concept, laying the groundwork for everything that follows.

In Chapter 1, we'll dissect the concept of purpose, providing a clear definition that goes beyond colloquial usage. Through examples from various sectors—be it business, social change, or even personal development—you'll see how purpose can manifest in diverse ways.

Chapter 2 shifts the focus to the significant role purpose plays in our lives and work. We'll examine the psychological and practical benefits, such as enhanced motivation, increased productivity, and greater well-being. You'll learn why understanding and articulating a clear purpose is not just a luxury, but a necessity for any successful leadership endeavor.

Finally, Chapter 3 offers a historical perspective, shedding light on how purpose-driven leadership has evolved over time. We'll discuss key figures who have exemplified this approach, as well as movements that have championed the concept. This historical context will enrich your understanding and appreciation of why purpose-driven leadership is more relevant today than ever before.

By the end of this section, you'll have a thorough understanding of what purpose entails, why it's important, and how it has shaped leadership models throughout history. This foundation will prepare you for the subsequent parts of the book, where we'll delve into how you can actively lead with purpose in various aspects of your life and career.

Chapter 1: The Meaning of Purpose

Welcome to the first chapter of this exploration into purposeful leadership. If we're going to delve into how to lead with purpose, it's essential first to grasp what we mean when we talk about "purpose." This chapter aims to dissect this often-nebulous term, breaking it down into digestible components so we can understand its full scope and impact.

Purpose is a term that has found its way into our everyday language, yet its meaning can vary depending on the context. Is it a lofty ideal that drives philanthropic efforts? Is it the driving force behind successful companies? Or is it the intrinsic motivation that fuels individual satisfaction and growth? The short answer is it's all of these things and more.

By understanding what purpose is and how it operates on multiple levels—individual, organizational, and societal—we can begin to appreciate its transformative power. Throughout this chapter, we'll offer clear definitions and delve into each layer of purpose. We'll also showcase examples from various fields to demonstrate how purpose has been effectively realized in real-world scenarios.

As you read through this chapter, keep an open mind. You'll find that the meaning of purpose is as diverse as the people and organizations who embody it. And understanding this is the first critical step toward becoming a purpose-driven leader yourself.

In leadership roles, purpose acts like the DNA of an individual or an organization, permeating every action, decision, and goal. When we talk about purpose in this context, we're discussing more than a set of objectives or a business strategy; we're talking about a core belief or philosophy that serves as the driving force behind everything the leader or organization does. This is the "why" that fuels your "what" and "how."

Imagine you are navigating through a dense forest. Objectives and strategies are akin to the map and compass you use—they help you determine your position and set a course, but they might change as circumstances evolve. Your purpose, on the other hand, is the reason you're in that forest in the first place. It's the end goal that justifies the journey, be it discovery, survival, or rescue. It doesn't change when you come across an obstacle or need to find a new route; it remains your ultimate destination, the fixed point guiding your way. This enduring quality of purpose distinguishes it from more transient aspects of leadership, such as short-term goals or specific tasks.

Purpose not only sets the direction but also deeply influences behavior. When a leader operates from a place of purpose, they are more likely to inspire commitment, foster a positive organizational culture, and make decisions that contribute to long-term success rather than seeking immediate gain. Employees and team members can sense when a leader is driven by a purpose greater than just profit or personal achievement; this often leads to higher levels of engagement and satisfaction.

Purpose serves as the touchstone against which all actions are weighed, and all decisions are made. It's the unwavering constant in the ever-changing equation of leadership. Whether you are making a difficult ethical decision, brainstorming innovative solutions, or simply communicating with your team, your purpose serves as the criterion that helps you make choices aligned with your deeper aims.

When we say that purpose is the core guiding principle in leadership, we mean that it's the root from which all other aspects of leadership grow—it's what makes leaders truly effective and impactful over the long term.

Understanding what purpose really means, particularly in a leadership context, requires us to delve into its multi-faceted nature. While the term "purpose" can be somewhat abstract, it becomes more comprehensible when we examine its basic building blocks: vision, mission, and values. These three elements not only help define what purpose is but also offer a structured approach to conceptualize and execute it effectively.

Starting with vision, think of this as your North Star. It's the grand, inspiring picture of what you hope to achieve in the distant future—be it five, ten, or even fifty years down the line. The vision serves as the ultimate destination, motivating you and your team to press forward even when faced with significant challenges. It's what you dream of achieving, the impact you want to make, or the legacy you want to leave behind. Vision transcends short-term objectives to provide a long-term focus that remains unaffected by immediate circumstances. It's that mental image of what success looks like for you or your organization, the one that makes all the hard work and sacrifices worthwhile.

Moving on to mission, if vision is the 'what' and the 'why,' then mission is the 'how.' Your mission is the blueprint for achieving your vision. It maps out the steps you'll take, the skills you'll need, and the impact you want to have on your stakeholders, whether they are employees, customers, or the community at large. While a vision might be lofty and inspiring, the mission gets down to the nitty-gritty. It's actionable, laying out a feasible pathway to turn your vision into reality. For example, if your vision is to revolutionize the renewable energy sector, your mission might involve developing cutting-edge solar technology and forming partnerships with government agencies. An effective mission not only outlines the plan but also energizes and inspires, reminding everyone involved why the vision is so crucial.

Values are the ethical backbone of your purpose. These are non-negotiable principles that dictate behavior and decisions. In the journey towards achieving your vision and carrying out your mission, you'll encounter various choices and challenges. Your values act as your compass, ensuring you stay on a path that aligns with your purpose. They help maintain the integrity of your vision and mission, providing guidelines for how to navigate ethical dilemmas or complex business decisions. For example, if one of your core values is transparency, you might prioritize open communication and honesty above short-term gains, even when being transparent is difficult or inconvenient.

By understanding these components—vision, mission, and values—you give yourself a framework for not just talking about purpose but also living it. These three elements intertwine to form the cornerstone of purposeful leadership, guiding you as you strive to make meaningful and lasting impact.

As we journey through the complexities of leadership, it's important to remember that these elements offer more than mere definitions. They serve as the operational gears in the machinery of purpose, each playing a critical role in manifesting what you stand for and aim to achieve.

When we speak of individual purpose, we're touching on a topic that is as diverse as humanity itself. Each person's purpose is a unique blend of their life's narrative, sculpted by various factors such as personal experiences, upbringing, culture, and even serendipity. Individual purpose is the culmination of what you believe your life is meant to accomplish or contribute. This might manifest as an artistic endeavor for one person, advancing medical research for another, or even something as straightforward yet profound as being a supportive parent or friend.

The notion of individual purpose often stems from an intricate tapestry of elements, encompassing life experiences that have made an impact, skills you've honed over the years, and values that are deeply ingrained in your moral compass. These factors come together to form a unique 'lens' through which you interpret the world, steering both your daily actions and long-term plans.

11

For instance, if your purpose involves social activism, then the career paths you consider, the community projects you engage in, and even the way you interact with your neighborhood would be influenced by that calling.

The role of individual purpose goes beyond merely shaping life trajectories; it infuses everyday moments with significance. When you live aligned with your purpose, even mundane tasks take on new meaning because they are steps on the path towards fulfilling it. You're not just going through the motions; you are part of a larger journey that you've defined for yourself. This sense of journey provides an underlying narrative arc to your life, turning setbacks into learning opportunities and victories into milestones.

Resilience is another key aspect influenced by individual purpose. Life is unpredictable, filled with both triumphs and tribulations. When you're rooted in your purpose, setbacks become less about failure and more about growth, as you're driven by a broader goal that supersedes any individual hiccup. This resilience often serves as the fuel that keeps the fire of ambition burning, allowing you to navigate life's complexities without losing sight of what you aim to achieve.

Individual purpose serves as the bedrock of your existence, anchoring you in a meaningful reality. It's the steady undertow that guides you through the ebb and flow of life's challenges and joys. It is this deep-seated layer of purpose that sets the stage for higher layers, such as organizational or societal purpose, to be built upon. The intimate nature of individual purpose makes it the cornerstone for any other form of purposeful existence, serving both as a starting point and a continual reference as you engage with the world in various capacities.

The concept of organizational purpose is a multifaceted one that invites a deeper exploration. When we transition from discussing individual purpose to that of an organization, we enter a realm that involves collective vision, shared values, and larger-scale impacts. Unlike individual purpose, which is deeply personal, organizational purpose is communal. It must resonate not just with the leaders but also with the employees, customers, and even the society in which the organization operates.

Traditionally, an organization's purpose was often reduced to its profitability or shareholder value. However, contemporary understanding recognizes that an organization's reason for being encompasses far more than its bottom line. An effective organizational purpose is one that serves as a North Star, offering a constant point of reference for decision-making, resource allocation, and strategic planning. It should be a guiding principle that permeates through every department and function, from the C-suite to the front lines.

One of the most intriguing dimensions of organizational purpose is its interaction with the individual purposes of those who are part of the organization. This dynamic plays a crucial role in employee engagement, job satisfaction, and overall workplace culture. When there's a harmonious relationship between the individual's and the organization's purpose, it often results in a virtuous cycle. Employees are more motivated and committed, which in turn enhances productivity and innovation. The organization, enriched by a purpose-driven workforce, is better equipped to achieve its goals, which then creates a more fulfilling environment that continues to attract purpose-driven individuals.

This alignment isn't always seamless. Conflicts between individual and organizational purposes can arise, resulting in various challenges. This tension is not merely a theoretical concern; it can manifest in practical ways, such as ethical conflicts, decreased job satisfaction, or even increased employee turnover. For instance, if an employee who is deeply committed to sustainability finds themselves working for an organization that prioritizes profits at the expense of environmental responsibility, the dissonance can lead to significant internal conflict for the employee. Over time, this disengagement can affect not just the individual but also team dynamics and, eventually, the organization as a whole.

The potency of purpose within an organization also stretches beyond its walls. A strong, well-articulated organizational purpose can serve as a magnet for customers, partners, and stakeholders. In an era where consumers are increasingly making choices based on the values a brand represents, an organization's purpose can be a key differentiator in the market. Moreover, a meaningful organizational purpose often encourages a broader sense of social responsibility. It's no longer just about what the organization can extract from the community and environment but also about what it can contribute to them.

Organizational purpose is a complex construct that stands at the intersection of strategy, culture, and individual aspirations. It's not a static tagline but a living, breathing ethos that has the power to inspire, unite, and propel an organization toward meaningful impact. Through its synergies and tensions with individual purpose, it offers a rich landscape for exploring what it truly means to lead and be part of something larger than oneself.

Let's delve into the notion of societal purpose. This form of purpose embodies a sense of collective ambition and shared destiny, transcending individual and organizational bounds to focus on the well-being of communities, societies, or even humanity as a whole. Unlike individual or organizational purpose, which can be insular or specific, societal purpose deals with overarching themes such as justice, equity, and environmental stewardship. It's the arena where purpose becomes not just a personal or organizational quest but a societal mandate.

The power of societal purpose is most evident in its ability to unify disparate groups and resources for a common cause. The sheer scale at which societal purpose operates means that the cumulative impact can be monumental. When individuals, organizations, governments, and other entities coalesce around shared societal goals, the outcome can be genuinely transformative. Consider landmark moments in human history like the eradication of smallpox, the monumental achievements in civil rights, or even the ongoing global initiatives to combat climate change. These aren't the accomplishments of a single individual or organization; they're the results of many aligning their various purposes toward a greater societal aim.

One fascinating aspect of societal purpose is its recursive relationship with individual and organizational purposes. Societal purpose acts as a form of accountability, posing tough questions that compel introspection and inspire action. It serves as a higher-order litmus test, asking whether your activities and ambitions are in harmony or conflict with larger societal goals. Are you adding to the social good, or are you detracting from it? The answers to these questions can influence the way people redefine their individual purposes or the way organizations reshape their missions.

Societal purpose elevates the dialogue around the role and responsibility of each one of us within the broader community. It challenges the paradigm of self-centered ambition, pushing for a more holistic approach that considers the interconnectedness of all elements of society. This level of purpose requires thinking in systems, understanding cause and effect at a macro level, and adopting a long-term perspective that weighs the immediate gains against the eventual impact. Societal purpose, therefore, is not just aspirational; it's also analytical and strategic, demanding a multifaceted approach that encompasses empathy, foresight, and meticulous planning.

Furthermore, societal purpose amplifies the stakes, escalating the sense of urgency and the magnitude of potential outcomes. When you act in line with a societal purpose, you're not just improving your life or your organization; you're contributing to a legacy that could affect generations to come. It imbues individual and organizational efforts with a deeper sense of significance, elevating them from mere tasks to components of a grander scheme.

Societal purpose is the apex of purposeful existence, merging the personal, the organizational, and the collective into a unified, impactful force. It's a form of purpose that has the potential not just to change lives but to shape the course of history. It serves as the ultimate mirror, reflecting the sum total of individual and organizational ambitions, and as the most potent magnifying glass, focusing disparate energies into a beam capable of piercing the most daunting societal challenges.

In understanding the abstract concept of purpose, concrete examples can be instrumental. They offer a tangible look at how purpose manifests in real-world settings across various domains, from business and the social sector to individual leadership. Let's explore these three sectors to glean insights into how purpose can be put into action.

The concept of business with a purpose finds an embodiment in companies like Patagonia and Tesla. These companies stand as testament to what can be achieved when purpose aligns with business strategy, influencing every aspect of their operations from top to bottom.

Starting with Patagonia, the renowned outdoor apparel company has made environmental stewardship its raison d'être. Far more than a mere slogan, this commitment is deeply embedded in the organization's DNA. For instance, Patagonia's supply chain is meticulously scrutinized to ensure that sustainable practices are followed at every step, from material sourcing to manufacturing. They have also implemented the "Worn Wear" program, encouraging customers to repair their gear rather than buy new items, counter to traditional consumer culture that drives many businesses. The aim is clear: make quality products while causing no unnecessary harm to our planet. This shared sense of purpose doesn't just serve as a motivator for the company's team; it also fosters a community of consumers who are more than just customers—they are fellow advocates for the environment.

Shifting focus to Tesla, their mission is nothing short of a sustainable energy revolution. Conceived with the audacious aim of countering the devastating effects of climate change, Tesla began with electric vehicles but has since branched out into renewable energy solutions like solar roofs and energy storage solutions. Far from a utopian vision, this purpose acts as a catalyst for groundbreaking innovation, steering the company into technological realms previously considered unrealistic for a green energy firm. Tesla's open-source approach to patents illustrates this, inviting even competitors to share in their technology for the greater purpose of global sustainability. In doing so, Tesla is not merely a car or energy company; it becomes a spearhead for a much larger movement toward a sustainable future.

Both Patagonia and Tesla offer more than just products or services—they offer a vision for a better world. They attract a workforce deeply committed to their purpose, creating a self-reinforcing loop of motivation and dedication that pushes the companies to new heights. Moreover, their clear sense of purpose carves out a distinct brand identity that resonates deeply with customers, investors, and collaborators alike.

In the realm of the social sector, the role of purpose is perhaps most pronounced, acting as the foundational pillar upon which activities, initiatives, and long-term strategies are built. The Bill and Melinda Gates Foundation and Doctors Without Borders serve as exemplars, each with a distinctly focused yet expansive sense of purpose that permeates their organizational ethos and guides their work on both small and large scales.

The Bill and Melinda Gates Foundation, one of the largest private foundations in the world, has set forth an ambitious purpose: to improve healthcare and eradicate extreme poverty globally. This lofty mission is operationalized through a diverse array of carefully selected initiatives. For example, they invest heavily in educational programs aimed at equipping young people with the skills needed for a successful future. Their global initiatives are equally expansive, spanning from projects aimed at eradicating polio and malaria to improving agricultural techniques in poverty-stricken regions. The Foundation collaborates with a wide variety of stakeholders, including governments, academic institutions, and other NGOs, ensuring that their efforts are magnified through collective action. In essence, each project they undertake isn't just a standalone effort but a cog in a larger machine driven by their core purpose. This multi-dimensional approach ensures that their resources are not just generously allocated, but also strategically employed to create maximum impact.

Meanwhile, Doctors Without Borders (Médecins Sans Frontières) operates under the purpose of delivering emergency medical aid to those affected by conflict, epidemics, or natural disasters, irrespective of geopolitical considerations. Their mission transcends the conventional boundaries of healthcare, encompassing broader humanitarian aims like the preservation of human dignity and advocating for social justice. This expanded sense of purpose allows them to venture into places where many other organizations hesitate to tread. They often operate in highly volatile regions, sometimes risking the lives of their personnel to fulfill their commitment. The kind of professionals attracted to work for Doctors Without Borders are often those who share this profound sense of purpose. They don't just see their roles as jobs but as a vocational calling, willing to forego personal comfort for the greater good.

In both examples, the underlying purpose serves as a magnetic force, attracting not only financial resources but also human capital. The people who work for these organizations are often driven by a shared sense of purpose, further strengthening the commitment and efficacy of these institutions. This coalescence of individual and organizational purpose not only enhances internal cohesion but also amplifies the external impact, making these organizations formidable agents of change in their respective fields.

When discussing personal leadership shaped by a strong sense of purpose, it would be remiss not to delve deeper into the lives of Malala Yousafzai and Nelson Mandela—two individuals whose leadership has been transformative on a global scale, guided every step of the way by a profound sense of purpose.

Malala Yousafzai, the Pakistani education advocate, didn't choose her purpose; it chose her. Surviving an assassination attempt by the Taliban at a young age for advocating for girls' education, Malala could have easily retreated from public life. However, this life-altering event only fortified her resolve. Her purpose transcended beyond her own personal ambitions or safety; it was fueled by an innate desire to empower girls through education. Malala leveraged her harrowing experience and the ensuing international attention to elevate her cause to a global platform. As the youngest Nobel Laureate, her leadership style epitomizes how purpose can not only steer personal decisions but can also catalyze broader movements. Today, her influence is palpable, from the corridors of the United Nations to classrooms in remote villages, impacting policy changes and individual lives alike.

Nelson Mandela, the stalwart anti-apartheid revolutionary and former President of South Africa, offers another vivid illustration of purpose-driven leadership. His purpose was daunting yet unequivocal: to dismantle the deeply entrenched system of apartheid and build a new, unified South Africa. Mandela's purpose was his north star during the 27 years he spent in prison, sustaining him through periods of extreme hardship. After his release, the world watched to see what a man imprisoned for nearly three decades would do. Rather than embarking on a path of retribution, Mandela chose reconciliation, adhering steadfastly to his purpose. His leadership during the delicate transition period was nothing short of exemplary; he extended olive branches where others would have brandished swords, all in line with his purpose of fostering unity in a deeply divided nation.

The above individuals exemplify how a well-defined sense of purpose can serve as an indomitable force guiding a leader's actions and decisions, even in the face of tremendous obstacles. In both instances, their leadership was not a series of isolated actions but a sustained campaign, every move calibrated to further their ultimate purpose. Their stories provide compelling evidence of the transformative power of purposeful leadership, proving how individuals can serve as catalysts for sweeping social change when driven by a deeply ingrained sense of purpose. They underline the profound impact that individual leaders can have, not only in achieving their own objectives but also in inspiring countless others to find and act upon their own senses of purpose.

These examples across business, social sectors, and individual leadership demonstrate that when purpose is clear and genuinely integrated into one's actions and decisions, it becomes an unparalleled driving force. Whether it's igniting innovation in a corporation, focusing the work of a non-profit, or steering the lifelong efforts of an individual, purpose serves as both the compass and the engine, guiding and driving in equal measure.

In this chapter, we've traversed the landscape of purpose, exploring its multifaceted dimensions and significance in various contexts—from individual lives to organizations, and even extending to broader societal frameworks. We've seen that purpose is not a mere buzzword or a fleeting trend; it is a foundational principle that can guide an individual or an organization in decision-making, problem-solving, and future planning. By dissecting the elements that make up purpose, such as vision, mission, and values, we gain a clearer understanding of its composite nature.

We've also delved into how purpose manifests on different scales. On an individual level, it's deeply personal, often shaped by a blend of experiences, passions, and values, serving as a guiding light in everyday decisions as well as life-altering choices. In organizations, purpose can act as a unifying force that brings together various stakeholders—from employees to customers— around a common goal or ethos. On a societal level, purpose can serve as a mechanism for collective action, compelling us to confront and address larger issues that affect communities and nations.

Examining real-world examples across business, social sectors, and individual leadership, it becomes evident that purpose isn't a peripheral element but a core strategy. Companies like Patagonia and Tesla have shown how a strong sense of purpose can drive innovation and customer loyalty. Organizations such as the Bill and Melinda Gates Foundation and Doctors Without Borders demonstrate the gravitational pull of a compelling purpose in galvanizing action around pressing global issues. And figures like Malala Yousafzai and Nelson Mandela serve as testaments to the transformative power of purposeful leadership on a global scale.

Understanding the nuances of purpose is critical for anyone aspiring to lead effectively. Without a deep-rooted sense of purpose, leadership can become untethered, susceptible to the whims of external pressures or short-term goals. Conversely, a leader grounded in purpose not only stands firm in the face of challenges but also has the potential to inspire others and effect meaningful change. As we move forward, this understanding serves as the cornerstone upon which the rest of this book is built.

It's the essential first step for anyone committed to leading with purpose, offering a framework that can help inform more actionable strategies and techniques in subsequent chapters. So, as we proceed, let this foundational understanding of purpose guide us in exploring the many facets of purposeful leadership.

Exercise 1: Your Purpose Statement

Objective: To formulate a preliminary purpose statement that encapsulates what drives you, both personally and professionally.

Materials Needed:

A quiet space
Pen and paper or a digital document

Steps:

1. Reflect: Take 10 minutes to ponder about what you're passionate about, what you're good at, and what the world needs from you.
2. Brainstorm: On a sheet of paper, jot down words or phrases that come to mind as you think about your passions, skills, and the needs you want to address.
3. Draft Sentences: Try to form sentences using the words and phrases you've brainstormed. Don't worry about making it perfect at this stage.
4. Combine and Refine: Look at the sentences you've drafted and combine elements to form one or two sentences that could serve as your preliminary purpose statement.
5. Seek Feedback: Share your draft purpose statement with a trusted friend, mentor, or family member. Get their input on whether it feels authentic to who you are.
6. Revise: Use the feedback to make revisions.
7. Commit: Once you're satisfied, write down your purpose statement in a place where you will see it regularly.

Discussion Questions:

- How does it feel to articulate your purpose in a statement?
- In what ways can you imagine this purpose statement affecting your daily actions and decisions?

- Do you foresee your purpose evolving over time? If so, how?

By the end of this exercise, you'll have a guiding statement that can serve as a north star for personal and professional decisions. Keep in mind that this is a dynamic statement; it can and should evolve as you journey through different stages of your life.

Chapter 2: Why Purpose Matters

In the previous chapter, we delved deep into what purpose means, its various components, and its manifestations at different levels—from the individual to societal. However, understanding what purpose is, would be of little use if we didn't also grasp why it matters so significantly, especially in the realm of leadership. The essence of this chapter lies in examining the tangible impact of purpose on crucial areas such as motivation, productivity, and wellbeing. These areas are not merely peripheral benefits but central tenets that can dramatically influence the effectiveness of leadership and the prosperity of organizations.

Purpose isn't a mere feel-good concept; it has real-world implications that directly affect both people and organizations. By nurturing a sense of purpose, leaders can ignite motivation, foster productivity, and enhance the overall wellbeing of their teams and themselves. A strong sense of purpose can be the linchpin that holds various elements of leadership and organizational dynamics together. In this chapter, we will dissect how this seemingly abstract notion translates into concrete outcomes, contributing to a more motivated workforce, efficient operations, and healthier work environments.

As we explore each of these facets, we will understand that purpose serves as more than just a guiding principle; it is a powerful lever that leaders can pull to bring about tangible and positive changes. So, let's delve into the vital roles that purpose plays in shaping better leaders, thriving organizations, and more fulfilled individuals.

The role of motivation in any endeavor cannot be overstated, and when it comes to leadership, its importance multiplies. One of the most compelling aspects of purpose is its profound impact on motivation. To fully understand this relationship, we need to look at the psychological underpinnings that connect purpose and motivation.

In psychological terms, motivation often arises from a need—either to address a deficiency or to achieve a particular outcome. Traditional motivational theories often focus on extrinsic factors like monetary rewards or promotions. While these are important, they can be short-lived in terms of sustaining long-term motivation. This is where purpose enters the equation. Purpose taps into intrinsic motivation—the kind of motivation that comes from within and is fueled by personal satisfaction and the joy of doing something meaningful. It provides the "why" that makes the "what" more engaging. Purpose gives us a deeper reason to be motivated beyond just completing a task or achieving a specific target.

Incorporating a sense of purpose into one's leadership style does wonders for individual and team perseverance. When people are clear about the larger reason behind what they're doing, they are more likely to commit, even in the face of challenges or setbacks. For example, a team that understands its purpose is not just coding software but improving healthcare accessibility will approach their work differently. This deeper sense of meaning and relevance can significantly increase resilience and determination. The difficulties encountered become obstacles to overcome on a meaningful journey, rather than roadblocks that bring everything to a grinding halt.

The role of purpose in motivation extends to influencing a culture of accountability and ownership. When individuals and teams are motivated by a shared purpose, it creates an environment where people feel responsible for the outcome, not just obligated to complete tasks. In this setting, individuals take initiative, creativity blossoms, and there's a greater willingness to invest time and effort.

Purpose isn't just a lofty ideal. It's a practical tool that can be harnessed to fuel motivation, offering both the reason and the emotional resilience to persevere through challenges. By understanding and utilizing the relationship between purpose and motivation, leaders can create an environment where teams don't just function—they thrive.

The link between purpose and productivity is increasingly becoming the subject of research and discussion in organizational psychology and business management. Unlike traditional metrics, which often focus solely on financial gains, productivity in the context of purpose goes beyond mere numbers. It encompasses not just efficiency but also the quality of output and the propensity for innovation.

When we look at purpose-driven organizations, we often find that their productivity metrics outperform those of organizations driven solely by profit. In a purpose-driven environment, employees are not just clocking in and out; they are deeply engaged in their work, aiming to contribute to a larger mission. This intrinsic motivation we discussed earlier feeds directly into productivity. When people care about what they are doing, they tend to do it better and more efficiently.

Google's example stands out because it encapsulates the essence of a purpose-driven organization with high productivity. This tech giant doesn't merely operate with the aim to dominate the market or maximize shareholder value; its foundational purpose is to organize the world's information and make it universally accessible and useful. This ethos permeates every layer of the organization, affecting the kind of projects they take on, the way they interact with users, and how they engage their employees.

One of the most intriguing aspects of Google's approach is the "20% time" policy, where employees are encouraged to spend about one-fifth of their working time on projects that interest them but are not necessarily part of their job descriptions. This policy has led to some of Google's most innovative products, including Gmail and AdSense. In other settings, time spent away from prescribed job tasks might be seen as a loss of productivity, but Google's case proves the opposite. The 20% time serves as an innovation incubator, fostering creativity and contributing to the company's broader purpose.

Another interesting point is the way Google handles failure. When projects don't pan out, they aren't considered a waste but rather a learning opportunity, reinforcing the notion that the quest to organize the world's information will have its setbacks, but each one offers lessons. This attitude further energizes the workforce, as employees know that their efforts, whether successful or not, contribute to a greater mission.

Even Google's approach to data analytics and performance metrics is tied back to their core purpose. The metrics are designed not just to measure output but to gauge how well the work aligns with and contributes to the company's purpose. This ensures that productivity isn't just about doing more, but about doing more of what matters.

Google exemplifies how a clear, purpose-driven ethos can serve as a catalyst for high levels of productivity. Their purpose guides strategic decisions, fosters innovation, and serves as a motivational tool for employees. It's a real-world example of how purpose and productivity are not just correlated but deeply intertwined in ways that contribute to organizational success.

Unilever's Sustainable Living Plan serves as more than just a corporate responsibility initiative; it's a strategic roadmap that has fundamentally shaped the company's business model and operations. With its purpose clearly articulated—to decouple growth from environmental impact while increasing positive social contributions—Unilever has gone beyond mere compliance with sustainability standards to embrace innovation and operational excellence.

One of the most salient aspects of Unilever's approach is its commitment to creating sustainable product lines, such as "Love Beauty and Planet" and "Seventh Generation." These product ranges are not only eco-friendly but also meet consumer demands for sustainable options, thereby hitting a sweet spot between purpose and market viability. This isn't purpose as an afterthought or a marketing gimmick; it's purpose as a driver of product development and business strategy.

Unilever's focus on sustainability has led to significant operational improvements. The company has invested in energy-efficient manufacturing processes, reduced water usage, and minimized waste, all aligned with its overarching purpose. These aren't just ethical choices; they're smart business decisions that have resulted in cost savings and efficiency gains. For example, through its eco-efficiency programs, Unilever has reported substantial reductions in waste, water, and energy costs, driving both sustainability and profitability.

Unilever's workforce is another area where the company's purpose-driven agenda has had a tangible impact. Employees are more likely to be engaged and committed when they see their day-to-day work contributing to a larger, meaningful goal. This engagement is not just about job satisfaction; it directly contributes to productivity. A motivated, engaged workforce is more efficient, creative, and less likely to turnover, reducing the costs associated with recruitment and training.

The case of Unilever powerfully illustrates how a clearly defined and well-integrated purpose can serve as a catalyst for productivity gains across multiple dimensions—product innovation, operational efficiency, and employee engagement. It demonstrates that when a company's purpose is deeply embedded in its strategy and operations, the result is a win-win: social and environmental responsibility go hand-in-hand with business growth and operational excellence.

The impact of purpose on productivity is also observed in smaller scale organizations and startups. When the goal is something everyone believes in, work becomes more than just a means to an end; it becomes a calling. In such settings, productivity gains are not just the result of working harder but of working smarter. Employees in these environments often show higher levels of problem-solving skills, creativity, and adaptability.

The role of purpose in boosting productivity is multi-dimensional. It enhances efficiency, encourages innovation, and elevates the quality of work. When leaders understand the direct correlation between purpose and productivity, they can harness it to build organizations that are not just successful in the traditional sense, but also more fulfilling places to work.

The influence of purpose on wellbeing is a dimension that cannot be overlooked when discussing effective leadership and organizational success. Studies have increasingly shown that having a clear sense of purpose is linked to numerous psychological benefits, including improved mental health and emotional stability.

Let's start by examining mental health. When employees find purpose in their work, it tends to mitigate stress and anxiety, which are prevalent issues in modern workplaces. People with a strong sense of purpose have an easier time navigating the highs and lows of work life, because they see setbacks and challenges as opportunities to grow and contribute to a larger mission. This resilient mindset can be particularly protective against burnout, a phenomenon that has reached epidemic proportions in some sectors. A purpose-driven work environment helps people not just survive but thrive, even under pressure.

The emotional stability afforded by a purposeful life is also remarkable. Emotional stability is a key component of emotional intelligence, a quality that enhances not only personal wellbeing but also interpersonal relationships at work. When a leader or employee is guided by a well-defined purpose, they often exhibit greater emotional regulation and adaptability. This contributes to a healthier work atmosphere, reducing conflicts and enhancing collaboration, which, in turn, positively impacts the collective mental health of the workforce.

Moving on to work-life balance and job satisfaction, the presence of purpose can be a game-changer. The modern workplace often demands long hours, leading to an imbalance that can affect personal life and overall happiness. However, when individuals are engaged in work that they find purposeful, they are generally more satisfied and better able to draw boundaries that protect their personal time. It's not just about working less but working better, more efficiently, and with greater satisfaction. The sense of fulfillment derived from purposeful work often spills over into personal life, enriching it.

Moreover, job satisfaction isn't only about the tasks performed or the financial compensation received; it's deeply tied to the feeling that one's work is meaningful and impactful. In organizations where purpose is emphasized, employees often report higher levels of job satisfaction, which contributes to a healthier work-life balance. Satisfied employees are more likely to stay with the company longer, reducing turnover and the associated costs of recruiting and training new personnel.

In summary, the role of purpose in wellbeing is multifaceted, contributing positively to mental health, emotional stability, work-life balance, and job satisfaction. Leaders and organizations that prioritize purpose don't just elevate motivation and productivity; they also invest in the long-term psychological and emotional wellbeing of their people, creating a more sustainable, balanced, and fulfilling work environment for everyone involved.

The significance of purpose as a driving force in leadership is evident across multiple dimensions. Purpose serves as a potent catalyst for motivation, imbuing individuals and teams with a sense of direction and the tenacity to persevere even when faced with obstacles. It enhances productivity by aligning organizational goals and individual efforts, sparking innovation and operational efficiencies that propel the organization forward. Finally, it significantly influences wellbeing by fortifying mental health, emotional stability, and overall job satisfaction.

Understanding and embracing purpose is not a mere nicety or a fleeting trend; it's an essential element that underpins enduring success and fulfillment. For those in leadership roles, paying attention to the power of purpose is indispensable. It's not just about steering an organization or leading a team; it's about cultivating an environment where people can thrive both professionally and personally. The benefits extend beyond the walls of the workplace to impact the broader social fabric. Ignoring the role of purpose would not only be a missed opportunity but a disservice to the individuals and communities that leaders serve.

When it comes to wellbeing, the role of purpose is often underestimated, yet it's fundamental. Purpose doesn't merely impact what we do; it profoundly influences how we feel and how we handle the stresses and challenges of life.

Understanding purpose has a therapeutic effect on mental health, often serving as a buffer against depression, anxiety, and burnout. The clarity that comes with knowing one's purpose provides an emotional equilibrium, enabling individuals to navigate challenges with greater resilience and equanimity.

Furthermore, a clear sense of purpose has been linked to greater job satisfaction. When people can see the bigger picture and understand how their role contributes to larger organizational goals or societal issues, their day-to-day work takes on new meaning. They're not just clocking in and clocking out; they're contributing to something larger than themselves. This sense of meaningful contribution can significantly improve an individual's perspective on their work, transforming it from a mere job to a vocation. It increases employee engagement and, importantly, lessens the toll that work can take on mental health.

Purpose also plays a vital role in achieving a healthier work-life balance. When work is aligned with personal purpose, it's easier to set boundaries and prioritize tasks, both professional and personal. The drive to work excessive hours wanes when individuals realize that fulfilling their purpose doesn't necessarily mean burning themselves out. Instead, they see the value in replenishing their physical and emotional energy as a means to better serve their broader goals. In this way, purpose acts like a navigational tool, helping people find a middle ground between work obligations and personal responsibilities or passions, thereby enhancing their overall quality of life.

In sum, the wellbeing benefits of purpose are multi-faceted, affecting not just what we do but also how we feel. Whether through bolstering mental health, enhancing job satisfaction, or helping maintain a work-life balance, purpose serves as a critical pillar for an enriched, fulfilling life.

In this chapter, we've delved into the multifaceted role of purpose and its profound influence on motivation, productivity, and wellbeing. Purpose acts as a catalyst, elevating individual and organizational performance while fortifying emotional and mental resilience. It's not just a theoretical concept but a practical tool that fuels motivation, guiding individuals and teams to persevere even in the face of challenges. When incorporated into organizational strategy, purpose leads to heightened productivity, sparking innovation and streamlining efficiencies. Most importantly, purpose plays a crucial role in our emotional and mental wellbeing, enriching our work and life through a sense of meaningful contribution and balanced priorities.

Given its sweeping impact, paying attention to purpose is not just advisable but indispensable for effective leadership. A leader attuned to purpose is better equipped to inspire teams, drive change, and contribute to broader societal goals. Whether you're leading a team, running an organization, or seeking to make an impact at the societal level, a clear, well-defined purpose serves as your North Star, guiding your actions, decisions, and relationships. Therefore, understanding and integrating purpose is crucial for anyone looking to lead with authenticity, effectiveness, and lasting impact.

Exercise 2: Understanding Your Leadership Style

Objective: To gain insights into your inherent leadership style and understand how it can complement or conflict with your purpose.

Materials Needed:

A quiet space
Pen and paper or a digital document

Steps:

1. List Qualities: Write down qualities or characteristics that you think make a good leader. This could range from 'empathetic' to 'strategic thinker.'
2. Self-Assessment: Next, honestly assess yourself against these qualities. Use a scale of 1 to 5 (1 being the lowest and 5 being the highest) to rate yourself on each.
3. Ask for Feedback: Optionally, you could ask a colleague, friend, or family member to also rate you on these qualities to get an external perspective.
4. Identify Patterns: Look for patterns in your ratings. Are you consistently scoring high or low in certain areas?
5. Alignment with Purpose: Compare these patterns with your purpose statement from Chapter 1. Are there any conflicts or synergies?
6. Action Plan: Develop a short action plan for enhancing the qualities that align with your purpose and improving on or mitigating those that conflict.
7. Review: After a month of implementing your action plan, revisit your ratings and adjust your strategies accordingly.

Discussion Questions:

- Were you surprised by your self-assessment or the feedback you received?
- How do you feel your leadership style currently aligns with your defined purpose?
- Are there changes you can make to better align your leadership style with your purpose?

The purpose of this exercise is to offer you a clearer picture of your leadership style and its compatibility with your purpose. By aligning the two, you can lead more authentically and effectively.

Chapter 3: The History of Purpose-Driven Leadership

In Chapter 3, we delve into the rich and varied history of purpose-driven leadership. The aim of this exploration is to provide you with a contextual understanding of how the concept has evolved over the years, laying the groundwork for its relevance in today's world. While purpose might seem like a modern buzzword, the idea that leaders should be guided by something greater than themselves is as old as history itself. Understanding this lineage not only gives depth to our discussion but also offers insights into the future of leadership based on purpose.

From the teachings of ancient philosophers to groundbreaking social movements, the concept of purpose has been a cornerstone in shaping effective and impactful leadership. What can we learn from Sun Tzu's strategic mastery in "The Art of War" or from Machiavelli's cunning insights in "The Prince"? How did modern theories like transformational leadership and servant leadership incorporate the notion of purpose? And perhaps, most importantly, what lessons can we draw from key figures like Mahatma Gandhi or Martin Luther King Jr., who have left an indelible mark on history through their purpose-driven leadership?

As we journey through this chapter, we'll examine how the concept has evolved, been refined, and been implemented across different periods and cultures. This will include not only a look at the theorists who have written about it but also the leaders who have lived it. We will examine the social movements that have been catalyzed by purpose-driven leadership, helping us to understand the broader impact of purpose on society at large. By the end of this chapter, you'll have a comprehensive understanding of the historical dimensions of purpose-driven leadership, equipping you with the knowledge to contextualize and enrich your own leadership practices.

The concept of leadership and its inseparable tie to purpose is far from new, tracing its roots back to ancient civilizations where philosophers, strategists, and rulers pondered the elements that constitute effective leadership. In this section, we will dissect the views of ancient philosophers and their contributions to the understanding of purpose in leadership and delve into historical texts that have been foundational in shaping leadership theories.

Delving into the annals of Western philosophy, one finds that the very foundations of the idea of purpose-driven leadership can be traced back to ancient Greece. Notable thinkers such as Socrates, Plato, and Aristotle offered groundbreaking perspectives on what leadership should entail, elevating the discourse from mere governance to a purpose-driven pursuit of societal betterment.

Plato, in his seminal work "The Republic," introduced the concept of the philosopher-king, an ideal leader possessing wisdom and vision. This isn't a leader concerned merely with territory or treasure but someone who is driven by a profound sense of justice and the greater good of society. Plato's philosopher-king serves as an archetype for purpose-driven leadership, demonstrating that governance should transcend the myopic pursuit of personal or even political gain. Instead, it should aim for a loftier objective: the holistic wellbeing of the community.

Aristotle expanded on these concepts, particularly with his idea of "telos," the ultimate aim or purpose inherent in each individual and thing. He argued that the ultimate goal for human life is "eudaimonia," a term that goes beyond simple happiness to encompass flourishing and fulfilling one's potential. In the context of leadership, this Aristotelian notion proposes that a leader's ultimate purpose should not be merely to direct or manage but to create conditions conducive to human flourishing. This involves physical, intellectual, and moral dimensions, pushing the leader to think about policies, practices, and cultural initiatives that allow individuals under their stewardship to achieve a fulfilling and balanced life.

These early philosophic principles have lasting implications for contemporary notions of purpose-driven leadership. They suggest that leadership isn't just about meeting quotas or achieving short-term objectives. Instead, the measure of great leadership lies in its capacity to elevate those it leads, aligning organizational or societal goals with the broader human pursuit of well-being and moral integrity. The ancient philosophers compel us to think of leadership as a deeply purposeful endeavor, one intricately tied to the ethical and holistic development of individuals and communities. This legacy continues to influence modern leadership theories, making it vital for current and aspiring leaders to heed these ancient yet enduring insights.

Shifting our focus to the East, ancient China also holds a wealth of wisdom on the topic of purpose-driven leadership, especially in Sun Tzu's monumental work, "The Art of War." At first glance, this text may seem exclusively suited for military strategy, but its teachings have been adopted and adapted across a broad spectrum of fields, ranging from business to politics and even to personal development.

Central to Sun Tzu's teachings is the concept of strategic alignment with an overarching purpose. The text posits that every tactical maneuver, whether on the battlefield or in the boardroom, should be intrinsically linked to a larger, guiding objective. This unity of action and purpose ensures that all energies are focused and channeled effectively, thereby increasing the chances of achieving the intended outcome.

In Sun Tzu's view, understanding the purpose behind any endeavor is not just advantageous—it's a requirement for success. His work elaborates on how tactical agility can only be truly effective when guided by a strategic aim. It's not enough to respond to conditions as they arise; one must anticipate, prepare, and act in a manner that is coherently aligned with a larger purpose. This applies whether you're positioning troops on a battlefield or navigating a corporate merger. The principle remains the same: a clear, well-defined purpose serves as the North Star that guides decision-making and strategy.

Sun Tzu's philosophy thus adds another layer to our understanding of purpose-driven leadership. His teachings illustrate that purpose is not a mere accessory to leadership but an integral part of strategic planning and execution. Whether in military confrontations of ancient times or the complex organizational challenges we face today, the unifying thread remains: a clear, overarching purpose is essential for cohesive action and effective leadership.

Niccolo Machiavelli's seminal work, "The Prince," has often been the subject of heated debate, particularly because of its sometimes-ruthless counsel on leadership and power dynamics. While many remember the book for its controversial stance on ethical conduct, less attention is given to Machiavelli's underlying focus on purpose in leadership. Central to Machiavelli's discourse is the principle that a leader's primary goal should be the stability and prosperity of the state he governs. In his view, the means to achieve this end are secondary and can be adapted, even if those means include manipulation or coercion.

Machiavelli's philosophy centers on the idea that a leader's actions should always be in service of a higher objective. Whether one agrees with his ethical viewpoints or not, the emphasis on having a clearly articulated aim is consistent with what we understand about purpose-driven leadership today. Machiavelli's political theory places the state—or in contemporary terms, the organization—as the entity that needs to be preserved and strengthened. This focal point serves as the guiding star for all tactical decisions and strategies.

Interestingly, Machiavelli also touches upon the necessity for leaders to adapt and pivot in response to changing circumstances, yet he argues that these adjustments must always be made in the context of achieving the leader's principal aim. This underlines the point that having a guiding purpose not only allows for focused action but also provides a framework within which flexibility and adaptability can occur.

While Machiavelli's ethical premises may be debatable, his views on the importance of a defining aim or purpose in leadership are poignant. He illustrates that regardless of the means employed, the success of any leader—in his case, the prince—is profoundly tied to a well-defined and overarching objective, aimed at the greater good of the entity they are tasked with leading. This understanding further enriches our ongoing exploration of the integral role that purpose plays in effective leadership.

The ancient philosophers and strategic thinkers made it clear that effective leadership is impossible without a guiding purpose. Even though they hail from different cultures and periods, these thinkers converge on the idea that a leader should be driven by a goal greater than personal ambition. Whether it's the general wellbeing of society, the victory of one's army, or the stability of a state, the concept of a higher purpose in leadership has been an enduring and universal theme throughout history.

The evolution of leadership theories has seen significant changes, especially in the last century, where the focus has increasingly shifted towards more participative and inclusive approaches. Modern theories like Transformational Leadership, Servant Leadership, and the emergence of Corporate Social Responsibility (CSR) reflect this change and highlight the central role of purpose.

The theory of Transformational Leadership, initially introduced by political scientist James MacGregor Burns and subsequently developed further by Bernard Bass, offers a robust framework for understanding the mechanisms through which leaders can drive exceptional performance and cultivate meaningful relationships with their followers. At the core of Transformational Leadership is the idea that effective leaders go beyond the transactional aspects of management—like rewards or punishments—to create a vision that inspires and galvanizes their teams.

In the Transformational Leadership model, leaders are not just taskmasters or strategists; they are, more importantly, visionaries with the ability to look beyond short-term problems to envisage a future full of possibilities. They possess the unique ability to articulate this vision in a way that is not only compelling but also deeply resonant with the values and aspirations of those they lead. This vision becomes a collective endeavor, a shared purpose that transcends individual roles and responsibilities.

In this framework, the power of a well-articulated purpose becomes evident. Leaders and team members alike find themselves motivated by a higher cause, a raison d'être that extends beyond the scope of their day-to-day activities. The employees aren't just doing a job; they are part of a larger story, contributors to a grander mission. This alignment with a higher purpose infuses their work with significance, which, in turn, enhances their commitment, engagement, and ultimately, their performance.

This sense of purpose also acts as an adhesive, binding individuals together and fostering a culture of mutual respect, trust, and empowerment. In such an environment, employees are not just subordinates following orders; they are partners in a transformative process, a process that encourages them to grow both personally and professionally. Transformational leaders provide the guidance and resources necessary for this growth, further strengthening the sense of shared purpose and collective achievement.

Transformational Leadership encapsulates the quintessence of purpose-driven leadership by showing how a clear, compelling vision that resonates with team members can act as a powerful motivator. This vision or purpose serves as the compass that guides actions, decisions, and interactions, leading to elevated levels of commitment and performance across the board. It is an illustrative example of how purpose, when deeply integrated into leadership, becomes a catalyst for transformative change, not just within organizations but also in the lives of those who comprise them.

The concept of Servant Leadership, formulated by Robert K. Greenleaf, introduces a paradigm shift in the way leadership is perceived. Unlike traditional models, where the leader holds power over subordinates, Servant Leadership flips this script, positioning the leader as a servant to their team. This inversion serves as a radical departure from conventional top-down, hierarchical structures, creating an environment that prioritizes the needs and growth of team members.

In a Servant Leadership framework, the leader's primary responsibility is to the well-being and holistic development of their team. The leader is vested in nurturing the physical, emotional, intellectual, and even spiritual needs of team members, going beyond the parameters of the workplace to support them as whole individuals. The ultimate aim is not merely to achieve business goals but to create a sustainable culture where people feel valued, where their work has intrinsic meaning, and where they can grow both personally and professionally.

The focus of Servant Leadership is thus not on profit margins or business objectives in isolation but on the larger mission that the organization is striving to accomplish. This emphasis on purpose creates a sense of organizational commitment that is nuanced and deep-rooted. Employees find themselves aligned not just with a role or a task but with a larger cause that holds significant meaning. This alignment breeds a unique form of loyalty and dedication, as the team members are not just working for a paycheck or career advancement but are engaged in a collective endeavor that serves a broader societal or humanitarian objective. It encourages the development of leadership qualities among all members of the organization. By emphasizing empathy, active listening, and collective decision-making, the model creates an atmosphere where each individual is encouraged to contribute to the organization's vision. Leadership, in this setting, is seen as a shared responsibility, closely tied to the shared purpose that guides the team.

Servant Leadership exemplifies how a purpose-driven approach can transform the dynamics of an organization. It emphasizes the integral role of a clear and meaningful purpose in motivating team members, fostering a strong sense of community, and nurturing a commitment that goes beyond the nine-to-five workday. Its focus on the needs of the team aligns seamlessly with the organization's broader goals, creating a cyclical effect where the achievement of individual purpose contributes to collective goals, which in turn reaffirm and reinforce individual purpose. It's a synergistic relationship that is enriched and amplified by the incorporation of purpose into the leadership style.

The evolution of Corporate Social Responsibility (CSR) as an integral part of modern business leadership represents a significant shift in how companies define success. Traditionally, the primary aim of a corporation was to maximize shareholder value, often with little regard for other stakeholders. However, the rise of CSR in the mid-20th century marked the beginning of a more comprehensive and holistic approach to leadership, one that considers not just financial performance but also the organization's impact on society and the environment.

In today's business climate, CSR is no longer an optional corporate program but a critical element of business strategy and corporate identity. The global community, fueled by increased access to information and a more socially conscious consumer base, demands more from corporations than ever before. As a result, a company's social and environmental commitments have become significant indicators of its overall integrity and reliability. Many consumers now make purchasing decisions based on a company's CSR profile, and investors are increasingly looking at these practices as a marker of long-term sustainability and risk management.

CSR not only expands the concept of purpose in leadership but also adds complexity and nuance. A company devoted to CSR must balance a variety of objectives, from shareholder profit to environmental sustainability and community development. This often requires a multi-disciplinary approach, involving collaboration between different departments like marketing, human resources, and supply chain management to align various facets of the company with its overarching purpose. It's not just about philanthropy or community outreach programs; it involves integrating ethical considerations into the core business strategies and operational processes of the company.

This shift towards CSR has also led to innovation and has opened up new avenues for companies to differentiate themselves. For example, companies are investing in green technologies, ethical sourcing, and inclusive hiring practices, which not only fulfill CSR objectives but also create a competitive advantage. Many organizations have also started to release annual CSR reports, disclosing their social and environmental performance to the public and creating a sense of accountability.

CSR therefore formalizes the broader ethical and social dimensions of purpose-driven leadership, creating a framework that guides companies in reconciling their commercial objectives with societal needs and expectations. It's a manifestation of a broader cultural shift towards ethical consumerism and responsible capitalism, where the onus is on companies to contribute positively to society and minimize their negative impacts. As such, CSR serves as an invaluable guide for contemporary leaders seeking to navigate the complexities of operating responsibly while still maintaining profitability. It highlights the deep interconnectedness between a company's purpose and its long-term viability, serving as a crucial link between organizational leadership and the betterment of society at large.

To encapsulate, modern theories have significantly expanded the concept of leadership, emphasizing the roles of inspiration, service, and ethical responsibility. These theories make it clear that an effective leader is one who is deeply aware of and committed to a purpose that extends beyond simple business metrics to consider the broader impact on employees and society. Whether it is inspiring transformative change, serving the needs of the team, or fulfilling social responsibilities, modern leadership is profoundly purpose driven.

The trajectory of purpose-driven leadership has been enriched by key figures who have personified its principles in various arenas— be it political, social, or business leadership. Their lives and actions offer invaluable lessons in leading with a sense of purpose that transcends personal or organizational gain.

Mahatma Gandhi is one such luminary, embodying leadership through nonviolence. A political and social reformer, Gandhi was not just fighting for India's independence but was committed to a greater purpose of social justice and equality. His leadership was rooted in the principles of 'Ahimsa' (non-violence) and 'Satyagraha' (insistence on truth). These principles were not mere tactics but a philosophical framework that defined his life's purpose. His concept of leadership was so potent that it not only mobilized millions of Indians but also had a lasting impact on civil rights movements globally. Gandhi's commitment to his purpose was unwavering, even when faced with severe challenges, and it's his leadership through nonviolence that still serves as a benchmark for effective, purpose-driven leadership.

In a similar vein, Dr. Martin Luther King Jr.'s life exemplifies leadership deeply entrenched in the quest for civil rights and social justice. The American civil rights movement under King was rooted in his deeply held belief in equality and human dignity, reflecting a compelling sense of purpose that went beyond mere political change. His famous "I Have a Dream" speech was not just rhetoric; it was a vivid articulation of his vision for a society free from racial discrimination. His leadership was transformative because it was fueled by a purpose that he believed was worth sacrificing for. The nonviolent protests and civil disobedience tactics he advocated were all aligned with his broader purpose, making him not just a leader but a symbol of a cause much larger than himself.

In the business realm, Richard Branson stands as an example of how entrepreneurial leadership can be harmonized with social responsibility. The founder of the Virgin Group, Branson is known for his unconventional leadership style that disrupts traditional business norms. His ventures, be they in music, aviation, or space travel, all contain a thread of social consciousness. Branson is known for prioritizing employee welfare and advocating for social causes, from climate change to human rights. His business acumen is tightly interwoven with his sense of social responsibility, making him a leader with a purpose that extends beyond profit margins. His commitment to various social issues demonstrates that purpose-driven leadership is not restricted to social or political activists; it is equally relevant and achievable in the business world.

These iconic figures—from Gandhi and King in the realm of social justice to Branson in the business landscape—highlight the diverse ways in which leadership can be purpose-driven. They show that regardless of the field, effective leadership is deeply tied to a broader sense of purpose. Their stories serve as compelling narratives that underscore the transformative power of leading with a sense of purpose, demonstrating its relevance across varied contexts.

Social movements have often been the breeding ground for purpose-driven leadership, creating platforms where leaders can effect monumental changes that align with their deeper goals. These movements themselves often act as collective expressions of purpose, rallying people around common objectives that transcend individual interests.

The Civil Rights Movement in the United States serves as an exemplary case study. This movement was not just about policy change; it was an uprising against systemic racial inequality that had plagued the nation for centuries. Leadership in this movement came from various quarters—religious organizations, educational institutions, and individual activists. Figures like Rosa Parks, Malcolm X, and, most notably, Martin Luther King Jr., emerged as leaders who were not just fighting against a law or a practice but were aligned with a broader purpose of social justice and equality. The movement was effective because its leadership was rooted in a cause that resonated deeply with a large segment of the population, both Black and White.

Environmental movements offer another domain where purpose-driven leadership has flourished. Whether it's the anti-nuclear protests, the fight against deforestation, or the modern-day campaigns against climate change, leadership in these movements has been characterized by a deep commitment to protecting the planet. Notable figures like Rachel Carson, whose book "Silent Spring" launched the modern environmental movement, or Greta Thunberg, the teenage climate activist, exemplify this. These leaders emerge from a shared sense of urgency and purpose—to safeguard Earth for future generations. Their leadership transcends political and social boundaries, making the fight against environmental degradation a global cause.

In the digital age, the open-source movement is a fascinating example of purpose-driven leadership in a non-traditional setting. Leaders in this movement, such as Linus Torvalds of Linux or Jimmy Wales of Wikipedia, aren't just creating software or online platforms; they're advocating for a philosophy of openness and collective contribution. The purpose here is to democratize information and technology, making them accessible to everyone, rather than keeping them confined to elite circles. This is a distinctive form of leadership where hierarchical structures are often blurred, and yet, the sense of purpose is powerful enough to mobilize thousands of contributors worldwide.

Each of these movements—Civil Rights, Environmental, and Digital Open-Source—demonstrates how purpose-driven leadership can arise in different contexts but always serves to unify, motivate, and inspire. The leaders in these movements are often ordinary people who choose to shoulder extraordinary responsibilities, driven by a purpose that promises a better future. Whether it's fighting for human rights, protecting the environment, or democratizing technology, these movements and their leaders serve as definitive proof of the power of purpose-driven leadership to bring about transformative change.

As we've journeyed through the annals of history to the cutting edge of digital innovation, one thing becomes clear: the concept of purpose-driven leadership is neither new nor confined to a particular era or sector. From the early philosophies that pondered the role of purpose in human life, through groundbreaking theories of transformational and servant leadership, to the societal movements that have shaped our world, the importance of purpose has been a constant thread.

Early thinkers like Plato and Aristotle laid the groundwork for the role of purpose in life and leadership. Centuries later, scholars and business leaders built upon these foundations to develop theories like transformational leadership, which centers on the idea of elevating mutual interests and focusing on the greater good. These modern frameworks moved leadership thinking away from mere transactional relationships towards a model where the leader's purpose aligns closely with the aspirations and needs of the people they lead.

While understanding this evolution is intellectually enriching, it's also practically essential for leaders today. The leaders and movements discussed in this chapter didn't just apply the concept of purpose to their causes or organizations; they lived it. They demonstrate that when a leader is aligned with a strong sense of purpose, they can galvanize groups, inspire action, and create lasting impact. It's this form of leadership that has driven seismic shifts in societal attitudes and systemic change in various aspects of life.

Ignoring the role of purpose can result in leadership that is not only ineffective but also potentially damaging, leading organizations and communities down paths that may generate short-term gains but are unsustainable and divisive in the long run. On the other hand, an understanding of how purpose has informed effective leadership throughout history can serve as both inspiration and guide for those aiming to lead in today's complex and rapidly changing world.

Delving into the history of purpose-driven leadership serves as a vivid reminder that purpose is a potent force. It not only drives individuals but also fuels movements and shifts paradigms. Today's leaders would do well to recognize this and integrate a sense of purpose into their leadership style, building on the valuable lessons that history offers.

Exercise 3: Evaluating Alignment with Organizational Values

Objective: To assess how well your personal purpose aligns with the values and mission of the organization you're a part of.

Materials Needed:

A copy of your organization's mission statement and values
A copy of your personal purpose statement
Pen and paper or a digital document

Steps:

1. Review: Begin by reviewing your organization's mission statement and values. Take note of key words or themes.
2. Compare: Now, look at your personal purpose statement. Are there any elements that directly correspond to or contradict the organizational values?
3. Rate: On a scale of 1 to 10, rate the level of alignment between your purpose and the organizational values. A score of 1 represents no alignment, while 10 represents perfect alignment.
4. Identify Gaps: If your alignment score is lower than you'd like, identify the specific areas where gaps exist. Is it a mismatch of values, goals, or something else?
5. Plan: Develop a list of actionable steps you can take to better align your personal purpose with your organization's mission and values. This could involve speaking with management, seeking out specific projects, or even considering a role change within or outside the organization.
6. Act: Begin to implement your action plan. Keep a record of any changes you notice in your level of engagement, satisfaction, or effectiveness.

7. Reflect and Adjust: After a set period, review your alignment score again. Has it improved? What additional steps can you take?

Discussion Questions:

- What did you discover about the relationship between your personal purpose and your organization's values?
- Were there any surprises?
- How do you plan to address any alignment gaps moving forward?

This exercise is designed to make you think critically about how your personal purpose fits within the larger context of your work environment. It offers a structured approach for identifying alignment gaps and creating a plan to close them.

Part II: The Framework of Purpose-Driven Leadership

As we transition into Part II of this book, we move from understanding the 'why' and the 'what' of purpose-driven leadership to focusing on the 'how.' While the first part delved into the importance of purpose and its historical evolution, this section offers a practical framework for implementing purpose-driven leadership in your own life and within your organization.

Chapter 4 will help you identify your own purpose, providing exercises and tools designed to clarify what truly motivates you. Knowing your purpose is the first step toward becoming a purpose-driven leader. It's the cornerstone that informs your decision-making, your strategy, and the culture you create for your team.

Chapter 5 then takes this a step further by showing how to align this personal purpose with your organizational goals. This chapter will feature case studies that illustrate the transformative power of purpose when it is effectively integrated into an organization's strategy. When personal and organizational purposes align, the effect can be profound, affecting everything from employee engagement to business performance.

Finally, Chapter 6 will delve into the art and science of embedding this sense of purpose into your team's culture. We will look at strategies and best practices for making purpose a lived experience within your organization. This is where the rubber meets the road: if you can successfully embed purpose into your team's daily activities, you can transform a set of individuals into a cohesive, highly effective unit.

So, as you delve into the chapters of this part, you will acquire practical tools and actionable insights to implement purpose-driven leadership effectively. Each chapter is structured to provide you with the framework you need to not only understand the importance of purpose but to live it, to incorporate it into your leadership style, and to infuse it into your organization's DNA. By doing so, you will be well-equipped to navigate the complex challenges of leadership in the 21st century, creating a lasting impact that goes beyond the bottom line.

Chapter 4: Identifying Your Purpose

Understanding one's purpose is like finding the compass that will guide every aspect of life, including leadership roles within an organization. Identifying your purpose serves as the foundation upon which you can build a fulfilling career and a meaningful life. While purpose may evolve over time, having a clear sense of it at any given moment will serve as a reliable guidepost, allowing for more focused decision-making, a stronger sense of self, and the ability to inspire and lead others effectively.

This chapter aims to equip you with a diverse set of exercises and tools that will help you discover or clarify your personal purpose. From self-assessment questionnaires to visioning exercises and advanced journaling techniques, these tools are designed to facilitate introspection and self-discovery. Our journey will also be enriched by case studies, demonstrating how identifying their purpose has helped various individuals transform their approach to leadership and life. By the end of this chapter, you'll not only have a better understanding of your own purpose but also possess a toolkit to help you maintain this understanding as you navigate the complexities of your career and personal life.

Self-assessment is the starting point in your journey to uncover your purpose. By taking the time to deeply understand your core values, passions, and previous experiences, you'll be in a better position to articulate what truly matters to you. Self-assessment isn't just a one-time activity; it's a continuous process that helps you align your actions with your evolving sense of purpose.

Questionnaires serve as a structured way to identify your core values and passions. These questionnaires often include a series of questions designed to tap into what motivates you, what you're good at, and what you consider to be most important. Some may include scenarios requiring you to rank your preferences or to choose between various values, such as honesty, compassion, or ambition. The goal here is not only to identify your values but also to prioritize them, which can offer invaluable guidance when you are faced with difficult decisions in your leadership role.

Reflective exercises on past experiences can also be illuminating. One useful technique is to consider significant moments in your life, both positive and negative, and analyze what they reveal about your underlying values and interests. For example, recall a time when you felt most alive or fulfilled. What were you doing? Who were you with? What values were you honoring in that moment? Conversely, remembering the times when you felt disheartened or disconnected can also provide clues about what might be missing or what you'd like to avoid in your purpose-driven journey.

Combining insights from both questionnaires and reflective exercises offers a comprehensive understanding of your core self. These foundational insights become the building blocks for identifying a purpose that is authentically yours, serving as a touchstone for future decisions, actions, and leadership opportunities.

Core Values Questionnaire

Instructions: Below is a list of values. Please read through the list and pick your top 5 values that resonate the most with you.

Integrity
Family
Innovation
Loyalty
Ambition
Compassion
Independence
Teamwork
Health

Financial Security
Follow-up Questions:

Why did you pick these values? Describe a situation where you demonstrated each one.
How do these values currently align with your personal or professional life?
Are there any values you wish to focus on more? Why?
Passions Questionnaire
Instructions: For each statement below, rate how much it resonates with you on a scale of 1 to 5, where 1 = Not at All, and 5 = Very Much.

I feel excited when I help others.
I enjoy solving complex problems.
Making money is important to me.
I thrive in social settings.
I feel fulfilled when creating something new.
Follow-up Questions:

What common themes can you identify among the statements you rated highest?
Can you recall a specific moment when you felt particularly passionate about something? Describe it.
How do your highest-rated passions align with your chosen values from the first questionnaire?
Completing these questionnaires should give you an initial understanding of your core values and passions. Remember, these are just starting points. The real value comes from deep reflection and ongoing self-assessment to develop a purpose that truly resonates with you.

Completing these questionnaires should give you an initial understanding of your core values and passions. Remember, these are just starting points. The real value comes from deep reflection and ongoing self-assessment to develop a purpose that truly resonates with you.

Reflective exercises can be a powerful way to understand your core values and passions better. Here are some exercises designed to provoke thought about your past experiences and what they reveal about your purpose.

Exercise 1: Peak Moments Reflection
Instructions:

Think about three peak moments in your lifetimes when you felt extremely proud, happy, or fulfilled.
Describe each moment in detail, capturing what happened, who was involved, and how you felt.
Analyze each moment to identify the values or passions that were present.
Questions for Reflection:

What similarities do you notice among these peak moments?
What values or passions were you honoring during these times?
How can you incorporate these values or passions into your future decisions?
Exercise 2: Life Timeline
Instructions:

Draw a timeline of your life and mark significant events, both positive and negative.
Next to each event, write down what value or passion was either honored or dishonored by that event.
Look for patterns. Are there certain values that consistently make an appearance?
Questions for Reflection:

What events stand out the most, and why?

Do you notice any recurring themes related to your values or passions?
How have your values and passions evolved over time?
Exercise 3: The 5 Whys
Instructions:

Think of an accomplishment you're proud of or a time you were particularly happy.
Ask yourself, "Why did this make me proud or happy?" Write down the answer.
Ask "Why?" four more times, each time going a level deeper.
Questions for Reflection:

What root value or passion did you uncover through this exercise?
Is this value or passion currently a significant part of your life?
How can you make this value or passion more central in your activities and choices?

These reflective exercises are designed to help you think deeply about your past experiences and what they reveal about your core values and passions. The insights gained from these exercises can be invaluable in identifying your personal purpose.

Visioning exercises can help you conceptualize your purpose and make it more tangible. Here are some methods to aid you in creating a personal vision and visualizing your purpose.

Exercise 1: Creating a Personal Vision Statement
Instructions:

Take some time to sit quietly and reflect on what you want your life to look like in 5, 10, or even 20 years.
Consider your career, relationships, lifestyle, and personal achievements.
Write down a statement that encapsulates what you see for your future. This is your Personal Vision Statement.

Questions for Reflection:

Does your Vision Statement align with the core values and passions you've previously identified?
What immediate steps can you take to start moving towards this vision?
How often will you revisit and possibly revise your Personal Vision Statement?
Exercise 2: Vision Board
Instructions:

Gather magazines, photos, or digital images that resonate with your purpose, values, and goals.
Assemble these images on a board or digital canvas.
Place the board somewhere you will see it regularly.
Questions for Reflection:

How do the images on your Vision Board make you feel?
What aspirations do they evoke?
Is there a central theme or message that emerges from the Vision Board?
Exercise 3: Guided Visualization
Instructions:
Find a quiet place where you won't be disturbed.
Close your eyes and take deep, slow breaths to relax.
Imagine a day in your life 5 or 10 years from now where everything has gone as well as it possibly could. Visualize your ideal scenario in as much detail as possible, from the place you live to how you spend your day.
Questions for Reflection:

What elements of this visualization felt most crucial to your sense of happiness and fulfillment?
How can you start incorporating those elements into your life today?

How did the visualization align with your previously identified values and passions?

Visioning exercises like these allow you to project your core values and passions into a future context, giving you a clearer idea of what you are working towards and why. Utilizing these exercises regularly can help maintain alignment between your actions and your broader life purpose.

Aligning your strengths with your purpose is a critical aspect of purpose-driven leadership. Recognizing your unique abilities can help you focus on areas where you can make the most impact. Here are some exercises to help you identify and align your strengths with your purpose.

Exercise 1: Strengths Inventory
Instructions:

Make a list of tasks or activities where you feel most competent or where others have complimented you.
Reflect on moments when you were particularly proud of your skills or when you felt highly effective.
From these reflections, identify your top five strengths or skills.
Questions for Reflection:

How often do you get to use these strengths in your current role?
Are there new ways you can leverage these strengths in alignment with your purpose?
Exercise 2: Strengths and Weaknesses SWOT Analysis
Instructions:

Create a grid for SWOT (Strengths, Weaknesses, Opportunities, Threats).
Populate each section with relevant attributes or circumstances.
Particularly focus on how your Strengths can yield Opportunities and mitigate Threats.

Questions for Reflection:

Can your strengths be used to take advantage of specific opportunities?
Are there weaknesses you should address to better align with your purpose?
Exercise 3: Align Strengths with Purpose
Instructions:

Take your identified strengths and your previously defined purpose or Personal Vision Statement.
Write down ways each strength can be applied to fulfill your purpose or move towards your vision.
Consider possible actions or roles that would allow you to utilize multiple strengths at the same time.
Questions for Reflection:

How does each strength contribute to achieving your broader purpose?
Are there new paths or actions that emerge from this exercise that you hadn't considered before?

By performing these exercises, you will gain a clearer understanding of how your unique skills can be channeled into actions that align with your purpose. This not only increases your effectiveness but also adds a layer of personal fulfillment and satisfaction to your endeavors.

For those who wish to delve further into the process of identifying their purpose, a range of advanced tools can be beneficial. These methods facilitate ongoing self-discovery and offer a more nuanced understanding of how various aspects of your life and career intersect with your core purpose.

Journaling Techniques for Ongoing Self-Discovery

Journaling is a potent tool for self-reflection, offering a platform to articulate your thoughts, feelings, and insights that might otherwise remain nebulous.

Instructions:

Set aside time each day to jot down your thoughts about your purpose and how your daily activities align with it.
Use prompts like "Today, I felt most aligned with my purpose when..." or "An obstacle to my purpose today was...".
Questions for Reflection:

What patterns do you observe over time?
Are there recurring themes or challenges that require attention?
Mind-Mapping Your Purpose Landscape
Mind-mapping offers a visual method to explore the many dimensions of your purpose, illustrating how different elements of your life and career are interconnected.

Instructions:

Place your identified purpose or core value at the center of a piece of paper.
Draw lines outwards to related domains of your life (e.g., career, relationships, passions).
Add further branches to identify actions, roles, or responsibilities in those domains that relate to your purpose.
Questions for Reflection:

Are there areas in the mind-map that seem underdeveloped?
Do new insights or actions emerge from this visual representation?
Conducting a 'Life Audit'
A Life Audit is an extensive review of your current life conditions and how they align with or detract from your overall purpose.

Instructions:

List various categories of your life, such as Career, Health, Relationships, and Personal Growth.

For each category, evaluate how well it aligns with your purpose on a scale of 1-10.

Identify actionable steps to improve alignment in categories that scored lower.

Questions for Reflection:

What categories require immediate attention for better alignment with your purpose?

Are there categories that you excel in, and how can you leverage that success into other areas?

These advanced tools are intended for a deeper dive into the complex landscape of purpose. They can help you continually refine your understanding, allowing for a more enriched and nuanced approach to purpose-driven leadership. By employing these methods, leaders can better align their actions and decisions with what truly matters to them, thus enhancing not only their efficacy but also their overall sense of wellbeing.

Case studies serve as compelling evidence that the journey to identifying one's purpose can have a transformative impact on leadership style, decision-making, and overall effectiveness. Here, we'll look at a couple of individuals who have successfully navigated this journey.

Oprah Winfrey: From Media Mogul to Purpose-Driven Philanthropist

Oprah Winfrey's journey to finding her purpose wasn't straightforward. While she found tremendous success in the entertainment industry, it was her shift toward philanthropy and empowerment that truly aligned with her deeper purpose: to uplift and inspire others. The Oprah Winfrey Leadership Academy for

Girls in South Africa and her numerous other philanthropic efforts are testament to her alignment with this purpose. After identifying her deeper purpose of empowering others, Oprah's leadership style underwent a transformation. She moved away from purely profit-driven initiatives to social impact projects, investing her influence and resources into causes that resonated with her purpose. The shift not only enriched her personal sense of fulfillment but also galvanized her large following to engage in more purposeful actions.

Elon Musk: A Vision for Humanity

Another individual who has effectively identified and acted on his purpose is Elon Musk. Known for his ventures like Tesla and SpaceX, Musk's overarching purpose is to ensure the long-term survival and progress of humanity. Whether it's sustainable energy or interplanetary colonization, each of his projects serves this grander vision, making him not just a business leader but a purpose-driven visionary. Elon Musk's understanding of his purpose has also informed his risk-taking and innovative leadership style. His drive to achieve milestones in human progress fuels his audacity to undertake projects that many would deem impossible. This clarity of purpose helps him inspire his teams, securing their commitment and driving them to achieve exceptional results.

These case studies demonstrate the profound impact that identifying one's purpose can have on their leadership capabilities. It becomes evident that when leaders operate from a space of clear, purposeful intent, their influence extends far beyond the conventional metrics of business success, reaching into realms of social and even global impact.

We embarked on a journey of self-discovery aimed at helping you identify your purpose in a meaningful way. The voyage began with an invitation to introspect through a collection of targeted self-assessment methods. The questionnaires were carefully constructed to prompt you to delve into your core values, beliefs, and passions—factors that fundamentally drive your decisions and actions. This served as the foundation upon which the rest of the exercises were built.

From there, we moved on to reflective exercises, encouraging you to tap into the wisdom that can be gleaned from your own past experiences. The purpose here was to enable you to connect the dots and recognize patterns in your life that point to your deeper motivations and drives. These reflective exercises were designed to be both analytical and emotional, aiming to engage your mind and your heart in the process of self-discovery.

Following this, the chapter introduced you to visioning exercises. These exercises were not mere daydreams but structured approaches to visualizing your life's purpose. We went beyond simply crafting a personal vision statement; the exercises were tailored to help you imagine the sensations, the challenges, and the triumphs that are part of your envisioned path, further clarifying and crystallizing what your purpose means to you in a tangible sense.

But understanding your purpose is just the first step. We also explored how to align this newfound awareness with your unique skills and strengths. After all, your capabilities are the tools that will enable you to manifest your purpose into reality. A set of exercises guided you through the process of identifying these skills and mapping them onto your purpose, thereby creating a roadmap for actionable steps you can take.

Recognizing the curiosity and complexity of human nature, we also dedicated a section to those who wish to venture further into the realm of self-discovery. Advanced tools such as journaling techniques were discussed to offer you a channel for ongoing reflection. Mind-mapping techniques helped to visually organize your thoughts about your purpose, and the 'Life Audit' presented a method for a comprehensive review of all the elements of your life in relation to your purpose.

Lastly, to emphasize the transformative potential of this process, we showcased real-world case studies of individuals who have successfully identified their purpose and have reaped profound changes in their leadership styles and lives as a result.

With this well-rounded toolkit, you are now better equipped to identify, articulate, and align your life around a purpose that is uniquely yours.

The process of identifying your purpose is a dynamic one, constantly influenced by new experiences, challenges, and insights. It's not something you do once and forget; it's a living, evolving guide that needs periodic reassessment and realignment. This chapter has provided you with a diverse set of tools and exercises to begin this journey. However, staying aligned with your purpose requires ongoing vigilance and commitment.

The importance of regular check-ins cannot be overstated. Just as you would assess the key performance indicators in a business scenario, your life too needs benchmarks for assessment. Setting aside time, perhaps as a recurring event in your calendar, can serve as an annual retreat for the soul. Revisit the self-assessment and visioning exercises, recalibrate your compass, and take stock of your progress and the alignment between your actions and your stated purpose.

The value of external perspectives in this journey is also significant. Engaging in deep, meaningful conversations with trusted peers or mentors can act as a mirror, reflecting whether your actions are in harmony with your declared purpose. These discussions can be eye-opening, offering you angles and dimensions you might have previously overlooked.

But the dialogue shouldn't stop with individuals you know and trust. Your environment—be it your workplace, community, or home—constantly sends you feedback, direct or indirect, verbal or nonverbal. Work evaluations, comments from friends and family, and even your own emotional state can be invaluable data points in assessing your alignment with your purpose.

Life is unpredictable, and the fluidity of human experience means your purpose can shift, morph, or even be completely redefined as you navigate through life's complexities. Adaptability isn't just permissible; it's a requisite for authentic, purpose-driven living. You need to give yourself the latitude to grow, change, and evolve, keeping your purpose attuned to the person you are becoming.

To make this iterative process more insightful, maintaining a dedicated journal focused on your purpose can be highly beneficial. This isn't merely a log of what you've done but a living document that captures your reflections, uncertainties, triumphs, and even failures as they relate to your purpose. This journal acts as both a historical record and a self-reflective tool, aiding you in staying true to your core motivations.

By adopting these strategies as part of your routine, you set the stage for a lifetime of leadership and decision-making informed by a deeply understood and regularly reaffirmed purpose. This enduring commitment to self-awareness and alignment not only enriches your professional journey but also brings a level of fulfillment and contentment to your life as a whole.

Identifying your purpose is not a one-time activity but an ongoing process that unfolds over a lifetime. As your experiences grow and your perspectives change, it's important to revisit the exercises and tools discussed in this chapter to ensure that you are still aligned with your original purpose or to modify it as needed.

- Regular Check-ins: Make it a habit to check in with yourself at least annually. Use this time to redo some of the self-assessment and visioning exercises to gauge where you currently stand.

- Peer Review: Sometimes, a third-party perspective can provide invaluable insights. Discuss your purpose with trusted peers or mentors to get their views on whether you're living in alignment with your identified purpose.

- Incorporate Feedback: Pay attention to feedback from your environment. Whether it's work performance reviews or candid conversations with family, feedback can often shed light on how closely you are living to your purpose.

- Adjust and Adapt: It's perfectly acceptable to adapt or even entirely change your purpose as you gain more life experience. What's crucial is that you remain authentic to yourself in whatever purpose you are pursuing at the time.
- Maintain a Purpose Journal: Continue journaling about your journey. This will not only document your progress but also serve as a reflective tool to ensure that you are staying true to your purpose.

Recommended Books and Articles

1. "Drive: The Surprising Truth About What Motivates Us" by Daniel H. Pink: This book explores the psychology of motivation and how it can be harnessed for better results in life and leadership.

2. "Man's Search for Meaning" by Viktor E. Frankl: A cornerstone text on the subject of purpose, detailing Frankl's experiences in a concentration camp and the lessons about human nature and the search for meaning.

3. "Start with Why: How Great Leaders Inspire Everyone to Take Action" by Simon Sinek: A look at how organizations and leaders can succeed by articulating and understanding their 'Why.'

4. "The Purpose Driven Life: What on Earth Am I Here For?" by Rick Warren: Though framed from a religious perspective, this book provides universally applicable insights into the quest for purpose.

5. "Good to Great: Why Some Companies Make the Leap...And Others Don't" by Jim Collins: This book details how companies can transition from being good companies to great ones, largely through leadership.

6. "The Art of Happiness" by Dalai Lama: A philosophical book that digs deep into the concept of happiness, a key component of finding your purpose.

7. "The Leadership Challenge" by James Kouzes and Barry Posner: A comprehensive guide to effective leadership, including how to align team goals with broader purposes.

Academic Articles: Journals like Harvard Business Review and MIT Sloan Management Review often publish articles on purpose-driven leadership and its various facets.

Online Tools and Assessments

1. StrengthsFinder 2.0: An online assessment that identifies your top five strengths, which you can then align with your purpose

2. Myers-Briggs Type Indicator (MBTI): A personality test that can help you understand your natural inclinations and how they might relate to your life's purpose.

3. Simon Sinek's 'Find Your Why' Toolkits: Available on his website, these toolkits help you articulate your individual or organizational 'Why.'

4. MindMeister: An online mind-mapping tool that can be used for plotting out your purpose landscape.

5. Penzu or Journalate: Secure online journaling platforms that you can use for the journaling techniques suggested earlier.

6. TED Talks: Websites like TED.com feature numerous talks on the subject of purpose, leadership, and motivation which can serve as useful resources for further understanding.

Utilizing a combination of these resources can provide a comprehensive framework to better understand and apply purpose-driven leadership in your life.

Identifying your purpose is akin to embarking on one of the most significant journeys of your life—a journey that doesn't really have an endpoint but evolves as you grow, both personally and professionally. Throughout this chapter, we've seen how essential it is to dig deep and get to the root of what really drives you. Various exercises and tools have been presented to guide you through this self-discovery process. But remember, these are not just checkboxes to tick off; they are instruments for ongoing introspection and alignment. As your circumstances change, as you mature and encounter new life experiences, you'll find that your understanding of your purpose becomes richer and more nuanced. It's not a static entity but a dynamic part of your life that will change and evolve, just like you do.

While identifying your personal purpose is an indispensable first step, the journey doesn't stop there. The next chapter will help you take this newfound or refined sense of purpose and align it with the broader objectives of your organization. As a leader, this alignment is critical for achieving both individual and collective success. We'll explore the avenues through which your unique purpose can be channeled to not only benefit you but also those around you—your team, your organization, and even the larger community. Through case studies and actionable strategies, we'll delve into how purpose can be deeply embedded into the very fabric of your organization's culture.

This interplay between individual purpose and organizational goals forms the core of purpose-driven leadership. When aligned properly, it can be the catalyst for incredible transformation, sparking not just improved productivity but also a more fulfilled, engaged workforce. The road ahead is exciting, and this is just the beginning.

Exercise 4: The Purpose Timeline

Objective: To visualize the evolution of your purpose over time and understand its origins, turning points, and future projections.

Materials Needed:

A large sheet of paper or a digital drawing tool
Markers, pens, or digital drawing tools
Your personal purpose statement

Steps:

1. Draw the Timeline: Create a horizontal line across your paper or digital canvas. Mark it with three sections: Past, Present, Future.
2. Plot Key Moments: Think back to significant life events that had an impact on your purpose. Plot these on the 'Past' section of your timeline. These could be personal milestones, educational experiences, or career shifts.
3. Identify Influences: Beside each key moment, jot down people, books, or experiences that influenced you at that time.
4. Analyze the Present: In the 'Present' section, write down activities or roles that are currently aligned with your purpose. Add your current purpose statement here.
5. Future Goals: In the 'Future' section, plot key goals or milestones you want to achieve that align with your purpose. These could be in the next year, 5 years, or 10 years.
6. Reflect: Step back and look at your timeline. Do you see patterns or recurring themes? Are there gaps or misalignments that you need to address?
7. Make Connections: Draw lines or arrows to connect related elements across different time periods. This will help you see how past events or decisions are impacting your present and could influence your future.

8. Adjust and Refine: Based on your insights, consider if your current purpose statement needs refining or if your future goals need adjusting.

Discussion Questions:

- What patterns or themes did you notice in your Purpose Timeline?
- Were there any surprises or "aha" moments?
- How has your purpose evolved over time, and what factors contributed to this evolution?
- Based on this exercise, do you feel the need to adjust your current purpose statement or future goals?

The Purpose Timeline exercise allows you to take a holistic view of your purpose, from its origins to its future trajectory. It provides a visual way to reflect, reassess, and reorient yourself as you continue on your purpose-driven journey.

Chapter 5: Aligning Purpose with Organizational Goals

In the previous chapter, we took an in-depth look at the essential task of identifying your individual purpose. The journey towards understanding your unique mission in life is a cornerstone of effective leadership. However, as critical as this individual purpose is, its power multiplies when aligned with the broader goals of the organization you lead or are a part of. This alignment is not just a bonus; it's a necessity for anyone looking to make a significant impact through their work.

Why is this alignment so crucial? The answer is simple yet profound: when your personal purpose resonates with the organizational goals, your motivation increases, your commitment deepens, and your ability to lead becomes more impactful. This harmony between individual and organizational purpose creates an environment where not just the leader but also the entire team thrives. But finding and maintaining this alignment is no small feat. It demands thoughtful planning, an understanding of organizational culture, and proactive leadership.

This chapter will serve as a comprehensive guide to achieving this alignment. We will discuss the step-by-step process for aligning your individual purpose with that of your organization and delve into the role of organizational culture in either supporting or hindering this alignment. Through real-world case studies, we'll explore how some leaders have successfully achieved this congruence and what we can learn from them. Additionally, we'll examine the strategies leaders can employ to facilitate this alignment for their teams. Finally, we'll identify some of the common pitfalls you might encounter and how to avoid them.

By the end of this chapter, you'll have a clear roadmap for aligning your purpose with organizational goals, setting the stage for effective, fulfilling leadership. This is a crucial next step in your journey towards becoming a purpose-driven leader. So, let's dive in.

The importance of aligning one's individual purpose with organizational goals cannot be overstated. This is a multi-faceted issue that goes beyond merely achieving a personal sense of fulfillment or job satisfaction. The act of alignment serves as a cornerstone for enhancing not only your effectiveness as a leader but also the overall productivity and wellbeing of your team and organization.

Consider, for a moment, the increased levels of engagement that come when people feel they are working towards something meaningful. When your individual purpose resonates with the broader mission of the organization, you become a more committed, motivated, and efficient leader. You're not just clocking in and out; you're invested in the work, always looking for ways to innovate and improve.

This sense of alignment has a ripple effect. As a leader, your enthusiasm and commitment are infectious, inspiring those around you to bring their best selves to the work environment. Teams led by purpose-aligned individuals often demonstrate higher levels of collaboration, problem-solving, and overall job satisfaction. In the modern business world, where competition is fierce and the rate of burnout is high, these qualities can set an organization apart, giving it a vital competitive edge.

Alignment with organizational goals creates a congruent work environment, in which actions and decisions are made in line with a clear, shared vision. This kind of alignment eliminates much of the friction and inefficiencies often found in organizations where individual and corporate goals are at odds. When everyone—from the top executives to the entry-level employees—is working toward the same overarching objectives, the path to those objectives becomes more direct and less fraught with obstacles.

Another important aspect of this alignment is its role in ethical decision-making. When your personal purpose aligns with the organization's, it often means your values are in sync as well. This value congruence makes it easier to navigate ethical dilemmas and strengthens the moral fabric of the organization, which is increasingly becoming a factor in consumer choices.

The alignment of individual purpose with organizational goals is not a luxury or an add-on; it's a fundamental requirement for any leader wishing to create a successful, ethical, and satisfying work environment. This alignment is what transforms routine organizational processes into a powerful movement that can change lives, disrupt industries, and even leave a lasting impact on society. It's the magic ingredient that turns a good leader into a great one.

The journey to aligning one's personal purpose with an organization's mission is a dynamic process that involves several key steps. Each of these steps is crucial for establishing a symbiotic relationship between what you as an individual are aiming to achieve and the broader objectives of your organization.

The Alignment Process: Steps

1. Self-Audit: Before you can align with your organization's mission, you first need to have a clear understanding of your own purpose. This may involve revisiting some of the self-assessment exercises discussed in previous chapters to clarify your core values, passions, and long-term goals.

2. Understand the Organizational Mission: The next step involves a deep understanding of your organization's mission, vision, and values. Go beyond the surface-level slogans and marketing

material—try to understand the 'why' behind what your organization does.

3. Identify Areas of Overlap: Look for points where your personal purpose aligns with the organization's mission. These points of overlap will be your primary focus areas, as they represent the opportunities for the highest levels of engagement and impact.

4. Communicate: Open communication is essential for effective alignment. Discuss your findings and observations with superiors and team members to get their insights and potentially identify other areas of alignment you may have overlooked.

5. Adjust: Based on these discussions and further reflection, you may need to tweak either your personal goals or your interpretation of the organization's objectives to achieve better alignment.

6. Implementation: Develop an action plan to live out this alignment in your daily responsibilities, projects, and interactions. Make it tangible and actionable.

7. Monitor and Review: Regularly review your efforts and adjust as needed. Keep an open line of communication with team members and superiors to discuss your progress and any new opportunities or challenges that arise.

Challenges and Obstacles

Despite the apparent benefits of this alignment, it's not without its challenges and obstacles. Here are some you might encounter:

1. Resistance to Change: Both individuals and organizations can be resistant to change, making the alignment process difficult. Be prepared to confront this resistance head-on, advocating for the benefits of alignment to both parties.

2. Misalignment of Values: There may be instances where your personal values and those of the organization fundamentally clash. In such cases, it's essential to consider whether the alignment is feasible or if it's better to part ways.

3. Limited Resources: Sometimes, the ideal alignment can be resource-intensive, requiring time and financial investments that may not be readily available. Finding creative solutions and demonstrating the ROI of alignment can be crucial here.

4. Conflicting Interests: You may find that aligning your purpose with the organization's mission puts you in a conflicting position with other goals or team members. Effective negotiation and problem-solving skills can be essential in these situations.

5. Evolving Purposes: Both individual and organizational purposes are likely to evolve over time. This dynamic nature requires constant monitoring and adaptation, adding a layer of complexity to the alignment process.

Understanding the steps involved and being aware of potential obstacles allows you to navigate the process more effectively. Alignment is a challenging but rewarding journey, one that can significantly enhance your effectiveness and satisfaction as a leader.

Organizational culture plays an undeniably important role in either supporting or hindering your efforts to align your personal purpose with the mission and goals of your organization. In a supportive culture that prioritizes overarching values, open communication, and engagement, it's much easier to integrate your own mission into the broader objectives of your team or organization. These workplaces offer multiple channels for effective communication and encourage proactive engagement from all members, making it easier to see where your personal and organizational purposes intersect.

On the other hand, in a culture that's either toxic or largely indifferent to broader ethical or social concerns, the obstacles to alignment can seem almost insurmountable. These are environments where short-term goals and individual competition are the focus, and the larger questions about organizational purpose and values are often ignored or dismissed. If you find yourself in such a situation, it can lead to disengagement, frustration, and ultimately, a sense of failure in your efforts to align your personal purpose with that of your organization.

Navigating this complicated landscape requires a multi-faceted approach. Building strong internal networks can be invaluable; the better your relationships within the organization, the more likely you are to find like-minded individuals who can offer insights and support. Open dialogue is equally crucial. Make the effort to initiate conversations around purpose and values, whether through existing channels of communication or by establishing new ones. Sometimes the organization just needs someone to take the first step to open up a dialogue around these issues.

By consistently demonstrating the added value that comes from aligning individual and organizational purposes, you make a compelling case for more widespread change. Tangible results often speak louder than any argument, and a track record of success can go a long way in encouraging a culture that values alignment of purpose.

Resilience and flexibility are key. You may encounter resistance, but it's important to stay committed to your personal purpose while also being willing to adapt your tactics. The ability to bend but not break is often crucial in affecting meaningful change, particularly in an established culture that may be resistant to new ways of thinking.

Sometimes, you'll need to escalate your efforts. In those situations, it's helpful to have advocates at higher levels within the organization who can push for broader cultural changes. It can be much easier to align your purpose with that of your organization when you have champions in leadership roles advocating on your behalf.

Remember that change often comes slowly, especially in larger organizations. Cultural shifts can take time and may require a sustained effort over months or even years. The key is to be patient but persistent, and to adjust your alignment strategies as the organization evolves.

Organizational culture is a dynamic and often complicated element that has a substantial impact on your ability to align your personal purpose with your professional role. By understanding the characteristics of your workplace culture and taking strategic steps to navigate it effectively, you can find ways to reconcile your own goals and values with those of your organization. This not only sets the stage for personal satisfaction but also contributes to the organization's overall effectiveness and success.

Let's delve into some real-world examples that demonstrate how individuals have successfully aligned their personal purpose with organizational goals. We are expanding some of our previous examples in order to show the applicability of the learning to a variety of aspects of purposeful leadership.

Case Study 1: Elon Musk and SpaceX

Elon Musk founded SpaceX with the grand vision of making life multiplanetary, a purpose that undoubtedly aligns with the organization's goals. SpaceX aims to revolutionize space technology with the ultimate aim of enabling people to live on other planets. Elon Musk's personal ambition fuels the company's innovative projects, from reusable rockets to ambitious missions aimed at Mars. The alignment between Musk's vision and

SpaceX's mission has propelled the company to be a leader in aerospace technology.

Case Study 2: Muhammad Yunus and Grameen Bank

Muhammad Yunus, an economist from Bangladesh, was driven by the purpose of alleviating poverty through microcredit. He founded the Grameen Bank, an institution that provides small loans to impoverished people without requiring collateral. Yunus' vision to empower the poor and provide them with opportunities perfectly aligns with the goals of the organization he created. His innovative model has not only proved successful but has been replicated globally.

Case Study 3: Malala Yousafzai and the Malala Fund

Malala Yousafzai survived a life-threatening attack for advocating for girls' education in Pakistan. After this incident, she co-founded the Malala Fund, an organization focused on advocating for girls' education around the world. Malala's personal experiences and passion for education drive the organization's mission. Through campaigns, research, and on-the-ground partnerships, the Malala Fund works to provide 12 years of free, quality education for every girl.

Case Study 4: Paul Polman and Unilever
Paul Polman, former CEO of Unilever, had a vision for a business model that not only ensured corporate success but also made a positive impact on the world. Under his leadership, Unilever launched the Sustainable Living Plan, aiming to decouple growth from environmental impact while increasing positive social impact. Polman's focus on long-term sustainability and corporate social responsibility was embedded into the company's broader business strategy.
In these real-life examples, you can see that aligning personal purpose with organizational goals creates a synergy that can be

extremely impactful. The individual leaders were not only able to fulfill their personal ambitions but also guide their organizations toward broader societal goals.

In examining the case studies of Elon Musk and SpaceX, Muhammad Yunus and Grameen Bank, Malala Yousafzai and the Malala Fund, and Paul Polman and Unilever, several common threads emerge that provide actionable insights for aligning personal purpose with organizational goals.

Shared Vision

In each of these cases, the leader and the organization share a well-defined, overarching vision. Whether it's making life multiplanetary, eradicating poverty through microfinance, advocating for girls' education, or promoting corporate sustainability, this shared vision serves as a guiding North Star that informs all strategic decisions.

Commitment to Long-Term Goals

Each of these leaders demonstrates a long-term commitment to their vision, refusing to let short-term setbacks derail their broader goals. Elon Musk's repeated rocket failures didn't deter him; Muhammad Yunus didn't back down when traditional banks refused to support his initiatives. This level of commitment sends a strong message throughout the organization, reinforcing the importance of staying aligned with its central purpose.

Inclusive Leadership Style

The leaders in these case studies not only have a strong vision but also cultivate an inclusive leadership style that encourages input from all team members. This approach helps to ensure that the workforce feels engaged with the organization's larger mission, further aligning individual purpose with organizational goals.

Innovation as a Vehicle

In each case, innovation plays a critical role in the alignment of personal and organizational purpose. From SpaceX's reusable rockets to Grameen Bank's unorthodox lending practices, these leaders leverage innovation as a way to make their vision a reality. By fostering a culture of innovation, organizations can better align their teams around a shared purpose.

Ethical and Social Responsibility

Lastly, each of these cases highlights a strong commitment to ethical and social responsibility. This not only strengthens internal cohesion but also resonates with external stakeholders, thereby enhancing the organization's reputation and effectiveness in achieving its goals.

Actionable Insights

Based on these commonalities, leaders can take several actions to better align individual and organizational purpose. First, they can work on clearly articulating a shared vision that both they and their organization can commit to. This vision should be ambitious but attainable, and it should serve as a guiding principle for all strategic decisions. Second, leaders should foster a culture of innovation and inclusion, where team members feel empowered to contribute their unique skills and perspectives toward the realization of the organization's purpose. Lastly, a commitment to ethical and social responsibility should be embedded into the organization's culture, ensuring that the pursuit of its goals remains aligned with broader societal values.

By examining these aspects closely, leaders can glean valuable insights into how best to align their personal purpose with that of their organization, thereby creating a more motivated, committed, and effective workforce.

Facilitating the alignment process between individual and organizational purpose calls for leaders to create an environment where a shared sense of mission is the norm. Open dialogue is fundamental in this regard. By incorporating regular discussions about the mission and goals of the organization into team meetings or one-on-one check-ins, leaders make everyone feel that their voice is heard and that their individual purposes can co-exist meaningfully with that of the organization.

Leading by example is equally important. When leaders embody the values and aims of the organization in their day-to-day actions, they inspire their team to follow suit. This commitment to a shared purpose reinforces that alignment isn't just optional—it's expected. Furthermore, this authenticity tends to bolster morale and encourage a deeper commitment from team members.

Skill development is another avenue for facilitating alignment. Leaders can encourage this by offering targeted training programs, rethinking job roles to better fit individual skills and passions or providing resources for personal and professional development. When team members feel they are growing in a direction that is aligned with the organization's goals, they're more likely to remain committed and motivated.

It's also essential for leaders to be adaptable in their leadership styles to fit the unique needs and challenges that arise in purpose-driven initiatives. Sometimes an authoritative style is necessary, but at other times, a more democratic approach that involves team members in decision-making proves to be more effective. The aim is always to keep the larger purpose in sight, regardless of the leadership style employed.

Celebrating milestones along the way is crucial for keeping the team motivated. The journey towards fulfilling any large-scale, purpose-driven goal will likely be long and filled with challenges. Recognizing and celebrating the smaller victories can offer immediate gratification and serve as a reminder of the larger purpose at hand.

Accountability cannot be overlooked. Leaders need to establish mechanisms like regular check-ins, key performance indicators tied to the mission, and open forums for feedback to keep everyone accountable to the shared purpose. Through a consistent focus on these elements, leaders can build teams that are not only committed to their roles but also to the larger mission of the organization, leading to both personal fulfillment and organizational success.

One of the most common pitfalls in the process of aligning individual purpose with organizational goals is the failure to communicate clearly. Often, this lack of clarity leads to misunderstandings about the mission of the organization and how individual roles contribute to it. The solution here is to establish regular, open channels of communication. Leaders should not just disseminate information from the top down but also encourage team members to share their perspectives and questions. This two-way communication ensures that everyone is on the same page and helps to prevent misunderstandings before they arise.

Another frequent issue is the misalignment of incentives. Team members may be motivated by different things—some by money, others by the potential for career advancement, and still others by the opportunity to make a meaningful impact. If the incentives offered don't align with individual and organizational purposes, team members may become disengaged. Therefore, leaders should endeavor to understand what truly motivates their team and structure incentives accordingly.

In some cases, organizations face the problem of an already established culture that may not be conducive to purpose alignment. Culture is not something that can be changed overnight. However, persistent efforts by leadership to promote values that align with the organization's purpose can gradually shift the culture in a favorable direction. The introduction of new rituals, the celebration of certain behaviors, and even changes in organizational structure can help in embedding a purpose-driven culture over time.

Even with the best intentions, there's a risk of overcommitting or biting off more than one can chew in the enthusiasm to be purpose driven. This can lead to burnout and a subsequent loss of faith in the purpose itself. The preventative measure in this case is pacing. Leaders should break down long-term goals into achievable milestones, focusing the team's efforts on manageable tasks while keeping an eye on the bigger picture.

The tendency to ignore dissenting voices is another pitfall. While alignment often results in a cohesive viewpoint, it's crucial not to marginalize those who offer different perspectives. Not only do these perspectives provide an opportunity for constructive debate, but they can also point out blind spots that may have been missed. Leaders should create a safe space for these voices to be heard and take their insights seriously.

It's also critical to note that the path to purpose alignment is not static; it's a dynamic process that requires ongoing effort. Leaders should make it a practice to regularly review the alignment between individual and organizational purposes, making necessary adjustments as the landscape changes. By being vigilant and adaptive, leaders can better steer clear of these common pitfalls and foster an environment where individual purpose and organizational goals not only coexist but thrive.

Measuring the success of aligning individual purpose with organizational goals is not a straightforward task, as it often involves both quantitative and qualitative metrics. Key performance indicators (KPIs) are essential for quantitatively evaluating alignment success. These can include metrics like employee retention rates, levels of employee engagement, and specific project outcomes that tie back to the organizational mission. The higher these numbers, the more likely it is that employees are aligned with the organizational goals, as they're not only staying at the company but also actively engaging in their roles.

Qualitatively, success can be measured through employee feedback and self-reports. Surveys and interviews can provide rich data on how well team members feel their personal purpose aligns with their work and the organization's goals. Open-ended questions can give insights into what team members value most and whether they feel these values are reflected in the organization's objectives.

The long-term benefits of successful alignment are manifold and significant. First, when employees' work is aligned with their personal purpose, they are more likely to be engaged and satisfied, leading to higher levels of productivity. In the long run, this can result in increased profitability for the organization. Second, alignment creates a stronger, more cohesive team. When everyone is working towards a common goal, team members are more likely to collaborate effectively, come up with innovative solutions, and support each other in reaching objectives. Third, organizations that successfully align individual purpose with organizational goals are generally more resilient in the face of challenges. When employees are deeply committed to their work, they are more likely to contribute constructively to overcoming obstacles, rather than disengaging or leaving the organization.

Overall, the long-term benefits of alignment can significantly impact an organization's success and sustainability. The advantage is not just in immediate, tangible outcomes but also in fostering a work environment where people are engaged, motivated, and committed for the long haul. Therefore, understanding how to measure success in alignment is crucial for leaders who aim to build and maintain a purpose-driven organization.

In this chapter, we've explored the multifaceted process of aligning individual purpose with organizational goals. We began by understanding the importance of this alignment and how it sets the stage for a more engaged, fulfilled workforce. The alignment process itself, while rewarding, is not without challenges. We've discussed the role of organizational culture and how it can either be a catalyst or a roadblock to alignment, offering strategies to navigate this culture for better congruence between personal and organizational objectives. Through real-world case studies, we unearthed actionable insights and pointed out common similarities that can guide future efforts.

We also touched upon the various strategies leaders can employ to facilitate this alignment. Recognizing and avoiding common pitfalls is essential for a smooth process, as is understanding how to measure success through both quantitative and qualitative metrics. These KPIs and other forms of evaluation not only guide the alignment process but also prove the long-term benefits of creating a purpose-driven organization.

As we wrap up, it's essential to recognize that the alignment process is ongoing. It's a constant dance of adjustment, measurement, and realignment. But the efforts are well worth the potential rewards, both for individuals and organizations.

Looking ahead, the next chapter will delve into embedding purpose in team culture. Now that we've laid the foundation of individual and organizational alignment, how do we make this part of the team's DNA? The focus will be on strategies, best practices, and actionable tips to ensure that purpose isn't just an organizational buzzword but a living, breathing aspect of your team's everyday life.

Exercise 5: Purpose-Goal Alignment Matrix

Objective: To identify how well your personal purpose aligns with your organizational goals and to develop a strategy for achieving better alignment.

Materials Needed:

A sheet of paper divided into four quadrants or a digital spreadsheet
Your personal purpose statement
A list of your organizational goals or objectives

Steps:

1. Label Quadrants: Label the top-left quadrant as "High Alignment/High Importance," the top-right as "Low Alignment/High Importance," the bottom-left as "High Alignment/Low Importance," and the bottom-right as "Low Alignment/Low Importance."
2. List Organizational Goals: Write down your organizational goals or objectives.
3. Rate and Place Goals: For each organizational goal, rate its importance to the organization and how well it aligns with your personal purpose. Place each goal in the appropriate quadrant based on these ratings.
4. Analyze High-Importance Goals: Pay special attention to the goals in both "High Importance" quadrants. If there are any goals in the "Low Alignment/High Importance" quadrant, think of ways you can either align them better with your purpose or reframe your view of them to see their value in the context of your purpose.
5. Consider Low-Importance Goals: Evaluate if the goals in the "Low Importance" quadrants need to be on your list at all, or if they can be delegated or restructured.

6. Create an Action Plan: For each goal in the "High Alignment/High Importance" and "Low Alignment/High Importance" quadrants, write down specific actions you can take to work toward them in a way that is aligned with your purpose.
7. Reflect: Take some time to think about what you've learned from this exercise. Do you feel more aligned with your organization's goals? Do you see areas where you can make changes?

Discussion Questions:

• Which organizational goals align most closely with your purpose?
• Are there any organizational goals that conflict with your personal purpose, and how will you address this?
• What adjustments can you make in your role or approach to better align your activities with organizational goals while staying true to your purpose?

This exercise should help you see more clearly how well your personal purpose aligns with your organizational goals and provide a pathway for bringing them into closer alignment.

Chapter 6: Embedding Purpose in Team Culture

In the preceding chapters, we navigated the journey from understanding the concept of purpose to aligning it with organizational goals. Now, as we move into the heart of organizational dynamics—team culture—it's time to focus on how to effectively embed this sense of purpose into the fabric of your team. This is a crucial undertaking because a team that is driven by a shared purpose is not only more engaged but also more productive and satisfied in their work.

The importance of a healthy team culture has been well-documented, but what sets this chapter apart is its emphasis on the intersection of culture and purpose. Far too often, organizational culture is mistaken for superficial attributes like office layouts or casual Fridays. While these elements may contribute to a sense of belonging, they don't necessarily instill a sense of purpose. True culture, the kind that elevates companies and drives legendary success stories, is about a collective vision. It's about shared values and goals, all of which align with a greater purpose.

Purpose is not just an individual pursuit. When integrated into a team's culture, it becomes a force multiplier, generating higher levels of commitment, engagement, and ultimately, performance. However, embedding this sense of purpose is not a straightforward task. It requires strategic planning, consistent effort, and above all, commitment from leadership.

In this chapter, we will delve into what team culture actually comprises, far beyond the surface-level attributes often discussed. We'll explore the methods for embedding purpose into this culture and examine the role of leadership in facilitating this embedding process. We will also look at the potential challenges that may arise in this journey and how to overcome them. We'll discuss how to assess the impact of these efforts and why the long-term benefits of a purpose-driven culture make this work so essential.

So, as you turn the page, prepare to understand not just why but how to make purpose the cornerstone of your team culture, setting your team—and your organization—on a path toward unparalleled success.

The fabric of what makes a team more than just a collection of individuals is the culture. Understanding team culture is paramount for any leader aiming to guide a team successfully. Team culture is essentially the shared values, attitudes, standards, and beliefs that characterize the members of a team and define its nature. It is the collective personality of the team and sets the tone for how members interact, make decisions, and accomplish tasks.

The impact of a team's culture on its performance and the satisfaction of its members can't be overstated. A well-defined, positive culture can serve as a powerful motivator and enhancer of productivity. It fosters a sense of unity and provides a common framework that guides behavior. When a team has a culture that aligns with its purpose and objectives, it not only helps individual members find their footing but also influences how satisfied and engaged they are in their roles. Consequently, understanding the current culture can be the key to successfully embedding purpose in your team.

Expanding further on the idea of team culture, it's crucial to note that culture isn't merely a tagline, or a set of guidelines outlined in an employee handbook. It's the lived experience of team members, expressed in their daily interactions, decision-making processes, and ways of resolving conflicts. In a sense, team culture is both a reflection and a shaper of collective attitudes—it echoes the prevalent mindset and influences future behavior.

Understanding this complex web is fundamental because a team's culture has a cascading effect on performance metrics, such as productivity, job satisfaction, and employee retention. A positive, purpose-driven culture often leads to high levels of engagement, lower turnover, and even increased profitability. On the other hand, a toxic culture can stifle innovation, hamper productivity, and make talented employees look for the exit.

Therefore, as a leader aiming to instill a sense of purpose in your team, understanding your existing culture becomes your starting point. Are team members cooperative or competitive? Is the environment open to diverse viewpoints, or is it constrained by a strict hierarchy? These are the kinds of questions that will help you assess the present culture and identify the areas that may need adjustment to align with your team's purpose better. Once you gain this understanding, you can then take targeted actions to mold the culture in a way that facilitates the integration of purpose into the team's DNA. By doing so, you'll be setting the stage for heightened performance, enriched job satisfaction, and a more harmonious work environment.

When it comes to embedding purpose into your team culture, a well-thought-out plan can make all the difference. Let's start with initiatives for spreading awareness. The first step is to make sure everyone on the team understands the larger mission they are a part of. This can be done through targeted communication initiatives like team meetings devoted to discussing the team's goals and how they tie into the broader organizational objectives. Leaders can also employ storytelling techniques to share compelling narratives that illustrate the purpose behind the work being done, making it relatable and inspiring for team members.

Another strategy to enhance awareness is to recognize and celebrate instances where team members have notably embodied the team's purpose in their work. This not only motivates the individual being recognized but also serves as a live example for the rest of the team, illustrating the type of behavior and accomplishments that are valued.

Moving on to strategies for internalizing purpose, one effective approach is to involve team members in goal-setting exercises that link individual roles to the team's broader purpose. This fosters a sense of ownership among team members and enables them to see the direct impact of their contributions. Employee involvement in corporate social responsibility (CSR) initiatives that resonate with them can also lead to deeper internalization of the team's purpose.

Additionally, one-on-one coaching sessions can be invaluable in helping team members align their personal career goals with the team's purpose. These sessions can be designed to identify any gaps between the individual's day-to-day activities and the larger objectives, followed by actionable steps to bridge those gaps.

Leaders should also make a concerted effort to weave purpose into the everyday experience of team members. This could mean starting meetings with a quick reminder of why the team's work matters, or it could involve more complex initiatives like establishing mentorship programs that align junior team members with more senior ones to work on purpose-driven projects together.

By using a combination of these methods, leaders can not only spread awareness of the team's purpose but also help team members internalize it, thereby weaving it into the fabric of the team's culture. This will result in a more engaged, motivated, and productive team aligned closely with both its own purpose and that of the larger organization.

When you're focused on embedding purpose in your team culture, the journey often begins with spreading awareness. First, you need to make sure that the team clearly understands the larger mission and purpose. Organize regular team meetings that are explicitly focused on this topic, giving people the space to ask questions and share thoughts. Use storytelling effectively to give context to the work everyone is doing, tying tasks and projects to a bigger picture that people can emotionally invest in. Public recognition within the team of those who exemplify purpose-driven work can serve as both reward and instructive example, creating an environment where the team's values are clearly demonstrated and applauded.

Turning awareness into internalization is the next significant step. This is where the rubber meets the road, so to speak. One effective method is to get the team involved in setting their own goals that align with the broader mission. This creates a sense of ownership and investment among team members. Also, encourage participation in corporate social responsibility initiatives or other activities that are in line with the team's purpose; this serves to deepen the connection between work and values.

Personal coaching or mentoring sessions can be transformative for individual team members. During these interactions, dig into the specifics of how each person's role aligns with the team's purpose. Offer guidance on how they can better align their work behaviors and outcomes with that larger mission. This could involve job crafting, where team members get to tailor aspects of their jobs to better fit their skills and interests, in alignment with team goals.

Never underestimate the power of daily reminders and rituals. Purpose should be a living, breathing part of team discussions and decision-making processes, not just an abstract concept that's talked about during onboarding or annual reviews. For example, start meetings by briefly discussing an element of the team's purpose, and look for ways to weave reminders into the team's day-to-day activities.

By adopting a multifaceted approach that involves both team-level initiatives and individual coaching, you create a rich ecosystem where purpose thrives. This positively impacts not only job satisfaction and performance but also the cohesiveness and resilience of the team as a whole.

Leaders play a crucial role in facilitating the process of embedding purpose into team culture. They are the ones who set the tone, creating an atmosphere that allows for a purpose-driven approach to take root. Through their own behavior, communication style, and decision-making, leaders can demonstrate what it means to be purpose driven. Their openness to discussing purpose, and their ability to link it back to everyday work experiences, encourages the team to internalize these values as well.

Leaders who excel in this aspect often employ an inclusive style of leadership. They actively solicit input from team members, encouraging a sense of ownership over the team's collective purpose. These leaders are often transformational in their approach, inspiring team members to see beyond the day-to-day tasks and connect with a larger mission. They are not just managers directing workflow; they are visionaries who elevate the aspirations of the entire team.

Another effective leadership style is servant leadership, which pairs well with a purpose-driven approach. Here, the leader focuses on fulfilling the team's needs and enabling their success, recognizing that the team's wellbeing and alignment with purpose are intrinsically linked. By meeting the needs of team members, leaders employing a servant leadership style create an environment where employees are more committed, not just to their role but also to the larger purpose that the team serves.

Some leaders find value in combining different styles to match the varying personalities and needs within their team. What's common across all effective styles, however, is the prioritization of open dialogue about purpose and an ongoing commitment to aligning team activities with that purpose. Regular check-ins, workshops, or retreats centered around team values and purpose can be instrumental in keeping the focus sharp.

So, whether they're applying a transformational, servant, or hybrid style of leadership, effective leaders take proactive steps to embed purpose within the culture of their teams. They understand that achieving a cohesive and resilient team culture rooted in a shared sense of purpose is not a one-off task but an ongoing commitment.

When it comes to embedding purpose in team culture, it's not always smooth sailing. Leaders may encounter various roadblocks that could hinder the process. Some common challenges include resistance to change from team members, lack of clarity in communicating the purpose, or the absence of resources to implement purpose-driven initiatives effectively. In some cases, the larger organizational culture might conflict with the team's attempt to foster a purpose-driven environment.

To overcome resistance to change, one of the most critical steps is open and transparent communication. Explaining the rationale behind the focus on purpose, and how it aligns with the team's and organization's goals, can go a long way. It's equally important to invite team members into the conversation, allowing for questions, concerns, and suggestions to be aired. Providing a safe space for dialogue can defuse resistance and enable buy-in from team members.

Lack of clarity in communicating purpose can be mitigated by revisiting and refining the messaging. Sometimes, bringing in external facilitators for workshops or team-building exercises can offer new perspectives and help clarify the purpose in a way that resonates with everyone. Utilizing various communication channels—meetings, written memos, one-on-one conversations—can also ensure that the message is both clear and reinforced.

Resource limitations require creative solutions. Even if there are budget constraints or time limitations, small, incremental changes can make a difference. For example, dedicating a few minutes in regular meetings to discuss how recent work aligns with the team's purpose can be a simple yet effective initiative. Leaders can also champion the importance of purpose-driven work within the organization to secure more resources.

If the challenge is a mismatch between team and organizational culture, that's a complex issue requiring a nuanced approach. Leaders may need to engage with higher-ups in the organization to discuss how a purpose-driven approach can benefit not just their team but the organization as a whole. Aligning the team's purpose-driven initiatives with organizational goals can also make it easier to gain broader support.

By identifying potential challenges early on and taking proactive steps to mitigate them, leaders can significantly increase the likelihood of successfully embedding purpose into their team culture. It involves not just the leaders themselves but the entire team—and often extends to stakeholders beyond the team, including upper management and even the whole organization.

Evaluating the success of embedding purpose into team culture is essential for understanding its impact and making future improvements. There are various key metrics that can be used to measure this success. These might include employee engagement scores, retention rates, or even specific performance metrics that align with the team's purpose. Surveys and feedback mechanisms can offer qualitative insights into how well the team's purpose is resonating with its members. Leaders can also track how often purpose is referenced or invoked in team discussions and decision-making as an indicator.

Beyond metrics, the long-term benefits of a purpose-driven team culture can be profound and multifaceted. For starters, teams that share a clear and compelling purpose are generally more cohesive, which in turn can boost productivity. A strong sense of purpose can also elevate the team's resilience, enabling it to better navigate challenges and recover from setbacks. Over the long haul, a purpose-driven team is more likely to attract and retain high-quality talent, as many people find greater job satisfaction in roles that offer more than just a paycheck. Additionally, the positive impact can extend beyond the team itself, influencing other teams and potentially reshaping the broader organizational culture in a positive way.

By carefully measuring both quantitative and qualitative metrics, and by being attentive to the long-term benefits, leaders can make a compelling case for the value of embedding purpose into team culture. This sets the stage for the next chapter, where we will delve into case studies that provide real-world examples of teams that have successfully made purpose a core part of their culture.

In this chapter, we've explored various facets of embedding purpose in team culture—from understanding what team culture entails and its effects on performance and satisfaction, to methods for making purpose a part of the daily fabric of team activities. We discussed the role of leadership in guiding this process, and how leaders can adopt specific styles to encourage purpose-driven initiatives. We also looked at potential challenges that could emerge and how to navigate them successfully. Finally, we outlined how to assess the impact of these efforts, using key metrics and indicators to measure short-term effectiveness and long-term benefits.

As we move to the next chapter, our focus will shift to the long-term sustainability of purpose-driven teams. We'll examine what it takes to ensure that a focus on purpose doesn't just create a temporary boost in morale or performance but becomes a lasting part of your team's DNA. From establishing ongoing training and development programs to creating a rewards system that reinforces purpose-driven behavior, the next chapter will provide a comprehensive guide for leaders aiming for sustainable impact.

Exercise 6: Purpose Mapping in Team Culture

Objective: To create a comprehensive map that captures the current state of your team culture and how it aligns—or doesn't align—with the purpose you've identified.

Duration: 60-90 minutes

Materials Needed:

Large sheets of paper or a whiteboard
Markers
Sticky notes

Instructions:

Brainstorm Current Culture Traits: As a team, brainstorm words or short phrases that you feel represent your current team culture. Write these down on sticky notes—one trait per note.

Map to Purpose: On a large sheet of paper, draw a circle in the middle and write your team's identified purpose inside it. Around this central circle, place the sticky notes from the first activity.
Arrange them in a way that shows how closely each trait aligns with the team's purpose. Traits that closely align should be near the central circle, and those that don't should be farther away.

Identify Gaps and Congruencies: Discuss as a team what you notice about the map. Are there traits that are closely aligned with your purpose? Are there gaps or traits that conflict with your purpose?

Strategize Alignment: For each trait that does not align well with your purpose, discuss as a team what could be done to bring it into alignment. Note these strategies down.

Commit to Actions: Turn each strategy into an actionable commitment. Assign a team member to each action and set a deadline for when it should be completed.

Review and Revise: Decide as a team when you will review this map again to measure progress. This ensures the exercise is not a one-time event but part of an ongoing effort to embed purpose into your team culture.
Debrief:

Discuss how the exercise felt, what was surprising, and what was affirming. Make sure to create a safe space where every team member feels comfortable sharing.

Follow-Up: Set a reminder for the team to reconvene and assess progress based on the deadlines set for the actionable commitments. This keeps the team accountable and provides an opportunity to celebrate successes and navigate any challenges that arise.

Part III: Leading with Purpose in Action

In Part III of this book, "Leading with Purpose in Action," we move from theory and preparation into the realm of practical application. Here, we dig into the trenches to explore how purpose-driven leadership manifests in everyday decision-making, team motivation, and crisis management. These are the litmus tests for any leader: the situations that reveal whether the purpose you've identified and embedded within your team culture actually translates into actionable results and long-term benefits.

In Chapter 7, we take a deep dive into the critical area of Decision-Making. How does a well-defined purpose influence the choices and actions of a leader? The decisions made by leadership don't exist in a vacuum; they impact the whole organization and its stakeholders. Here, we'll unpack how to make decisions that are consistent with your purpose, even when faced with complex challenges or ethical dilemmas.

Following this, Chapter 8 will guide you through the art of Inspiring Your Team. A leader's influence extends beyond decision-making and into the realm of human emotion and motivation. A leader's vision should be compelling enough to inspire a team to action. But how can this be achieved? What are the tools and techniques that can help motivate a team towards a shared purpose?

In Chapter 9 we delve into Handling Challenges. Leading with purpose is not just about the easy times; it's also about steering the ship in rough seas. During crises, a clearly defined purpose can serve as a guiding light, offering a sense of direction when the way forward is murky. Here we explore the robustness of purpose-driven leadership, especially in times when it's most needed.

As we progress through these next chapters, you'll learn not just the 'what' and the 'why' but also the 'how' of leading with purpose.

This section aims to equip you with actionable strategies and insights that will transform your leadership from aspirational to operational. Prepare yourself; it's time to lead with purpose in action.

Chapter 7: Decision-Making

As we venture into the next phase of our journey in understanding purpose-driven leadership, we come to a critical juncture: the role of decision-making. The ability to make sound choices serves as the linchpin of effective leadership, affecting not only the leader but also the team and the broader organization. Decision-making isn't just a matter of weighing pros and cons, flipping coins, or even gut instinct. At its most impactful, decision-making is guided by a well-defined purpose, which acts like a compass during times of uncertainty.

The premise is simple yet powerful: When you are clear about your purpose, you can make decisions that are aligned with your core values and the overarching goals of your organization. Such alignment does more than just simplify the decision-making process; it infuses each choice with meaning, thereby increasing the likelihood of success while also making the outcomes more fulfilling for all involved.

This chapter aims to delve into the complex labyrinth of decision-making, examining how a clearly defined purpose can serve as your guide. We will discuss the intricate processes that go into making a decision and how you can ensure that your choices are not only effective but also ethically sound and aligned with the interests of all stakeholders involved. Through case studies, we will explore real-world examples that demonstrate the transformative power of purpose-driven decision-making. We will also introduce you to various decision-making models and frameworks that can be adapted to incorporate purpose as a central element.

Decision-making without a purpose is like sailing without a compass; you may move, but you'll lack direction. This chapter offers you the tools you need to ensure that each decision you make is a step in the right direction, aligned with your purpose and that of your organization. And as you'll find in the next chapters, decision-making is but the first in a series of actionable strategies for implementing purpose-driven leadership in various aspects of your professional life.

The decision-making process is a multifaceted endeavor that often involves a series of steps and considerations. Traditional decision-making models might have you identify the problem, gather information, consider the options, weigh the pros and cons, make a choice, and then evaluate the outcome. While these steps provide a foundational framework, the incorporation of purpose adds a rich, meaningful layer to the process that cannot be ignored for effective and ethical leadership.

In the initial stage of identifying the problem or opportunity, purpose can serve as a lens through which to view the situation. Rather than just seeing a challenge to be solved or a goal to be achieved, align the issue with your personal and organizational purpose. Ask yourself how solving this problem or seizing this opportunity resonates with the values and objectives that you and your organization hold dear.

Once you move on to gathering information, ensure that your sources and methods are in line with your purpose. For example, if your organizational purpose is sustainability, you'd focus on collecting data that takes into account not just financial profitability but also environmental and social impacts.

When it comes to evaluating options, purpose once again plays a pivotal role. A decision aligned with purpose often transcends the obvious immediate benefits, offering long-term advantages that may not be immediately apparent. Here, the use of purpose allows you to employ a more comprehensive set of criteria for evaluation, thereby often leading to more innovative and impactful solutions.

In the decision-making stage, the clarity of purpose can be the deciding factor among options that seem otherwise equally viable. The chosen path should not only solve the problem at hand but also further the mission and values you're committed to. Sometimes, this may even mean choosing a more difficult or less profitable route in the short term for long-term alignment with your purpose.

When evaluating the results, it's important to measure not just tangible outcomes but also how the decision has moved you and your organization closer to fulfilling your shared purpose. It might also involve recalibrating your strategies for future decisions based on this assessment.

Incorporating purpose into each step of the decision-making process elevates the exercise from a mere problem-solving task to a transformative experience. It offers a more nuanced and comprehensive approach, providing not just a solution, but a meaningful contribution to a larger mission.

Ethical considerations are indispensable in the decision-making process, especially when aiming to lead with purpose. Ethics serve as the moral compass that guides actions and choices, ensuring that they are not only effective but also just, fair, and aligned with broader societal values. When ethics and purpose converge in decision-making, the outcome often surpasses the immediate organizational goals to create a lasting, positive impact on stakeholders and communities.

The importance of ethics manifests right from the first stage of identifying the problem or opportunity. Here, ethical considerations will prompt you to ask questions about the fairness, inclusivity, and potential consequences of the options before you. These questions are not merely legal stipulations or corporate compliance checks; they are vital inquiries that help align the decision with the organizational purpose. For instance, if your organization's purpose includes sustainability, ethical considerations would involve scrutinizing the environmental footprint of your potential choices.

When gathering information, ethics and purpose go hand in hand to determine the kind of data that is relevant and how it is obtained. Ethical considerations ensure that the information is gathered transparently and responsibly, respecting privacy laws, and without manipulating or coercing sources. Aligning these ethical practices with organizational purpose ensures that the data gathered will be not only accurate but also meaningful in the broader context of your mission.

The evaluation of options must also be ethical. This entails scrutinizing each option for its potential impact on all stakeholders, not just the bottom line. An ethically sound, purpose-driven evaluation will consider the long-term consequences of each decision, including its social, environmental, and economic ramifications. This makes the decision-making process not just an organizational activity, but a societal one.

Ethics should be at the forefront when the actual decision is made. An ethically made decision is one that you can proudly stand by, knowing that you have not compromised your values or those of your organization. Ethics and purpose together can act as a strong filter, helping to eliminate options that may seem lucrative in the short term but are misaligned with your long-term mission and values.

During the evaluation of the outcomes, ethical considerations provide an additional layer of assessment. Beyond asking whether the decision achieved its intended goals, you assess whether it did so in a manner that was fair, just, and aligned with both ethical guidelines and organizational purpose.

Ethics are not a separate component but rather integrated into each step of purpose-driven decision-making. They ensure that the actions taken are congruent with the values and long-term objectives that define your organization's purpose, thereby elevating the quality and impact of your decisions.

Balancing stakeholder interests is a complex but vital aspect of purpose-driven decision-making. Stakeholders can include a diverse array of individuals and entities, from employees and customers to investors, regulatory bodies, and the communities in which the organization operates. Their interests may not always align seamlessly with each other or with the overarching purpose of the organization. Therefore, thoughtful strategies must be applied to ensure that decisions serve a balanced benefit.

The first step in this endeavor is to identify who the key stakeholders are. This requires an expansive view of influence and impact. It goes beyond the usual suspects like shareholders who might be most vocal or have direct financial stakes. Consideration should also be given to community members affected by organizational activities, industry partners, and even future generations that might be impacted by long-term decisions, especially those relating to environmental sustainability.

After identifying the key stakeholders, the next step involves understanding their interests, concerns, and expectations. This might require open dialogues, surveys, or community engagement initiatives to gather qualitative and quantitative data. A careful analysis of this data will not only reveal what stakeholders value most but also identify common ground where their interests overlap with the organizational purpose.

When it comes to making the actual decision, this collected data is invaluable. Leaders should map out how each option aligns with stakeholder interests and the organization's purpose. In some cases, trade-offs may be unavoidable. Here, transparency is crucial. Being open about the decision-making process and the reasons for certain trade-offs not only maintains trust but can also provide stakeholders with a broader understanding of the organizational objectives.

It's also important to loop back with stakeholders after decisions are implemented. This evaluation phase involves measuring the impact of the decisions to see if they achieved the desired outcomes and how they affected stakeholders. This feedback loop is not only a good governance practice but also provides important insights for future decision-making.

Balancing stakeholder interests is not a side activity but a central component of purpose-driven decision-making. It involves thorough identification, engagement, and analysis of stakeholder interests and a careful alignment of these interests with the organizational purpose at every stage of the decision-making process. This ensures that decisions are not only effective but also equitable, thereby strengthening the purpose-driven foundation of the organization. Let's turn now to some case studies that illustrate the importance of decision making in purpose driven leadership.

Case Study 1: Patagonia's Decision to Donate Black Friday Profits

In 2016, outdoor clothing company Patagonia decided to donate 100% of its Black Friday sales to grassroots environmental organizations. This bold decision aligned seamlessly with Patagonia's overarching purpose of being a leader in sustainable business practices and environmental conservation. Not only did this action generate positive public relations, but the company also saw an unprecedented surge in sales, pulling in $10 million—five times the expected amount. Aligning bold decisions with organizational purpose can result in unexpected benefits, both in terms of reputation and financial gain. A well-executed strategy that aligns with purpose can turn a standard business operation, like a Black Friday sale, into a powerful tool for change.

Case Study 2: CVS Health Stops Selling Tobacco

In 2014, CVS Health made the radical decision to stop selling tobacco products in its stores, sacrificing $2 billion in annual sales. This decision aligned with the company's purpose of helping people on their path to better health. The move was initially met with skepticism, but it improved CVS Health's brand reputation and attracted new partnerships, including a long-term contract with the American Heart Association. Even decisions that result in short-term financial loss can lead to long-term gains in brand value and stakeholder trust. Consistency between an organization's purpose and its actions can create opportunities for meaningful partnerships and alliances.

Case Study 3: Microsoft's Investment in Renewable Energy

Microsoft's commitment to sustainability was solidified when the company decided to invest in renewable energy options for their data centers. This commitment is not only in line with reducing carbon footprint but also resonates with their broader purpose of empowering individuals and organizations to achieve more—a more sustainable future in this context. Purpose-driven decision-making in resource-intensive areas of a business can have a cascading effect on the entire supply chain, prompting other stakeholders to adopt similar practices. Establishing a purpose that goes beyond the immediate interests of the company can foster a culture of responsibility and provide a competitive edge in attracting like-minded customers and partners.

Each of these case studies demonstrates the transformative power of purpose-driven decision-making. Whether it's sacrificing immediate profits for long-term gain or turning traditional business operations into purpose-driven initiatives, the impact of these decisions extends far beyond the bottom line. They shape brand identities, forge meaningful partnerships, and set new standards for entire industries.

Decision-making models offer structured ways to approach choices in business and personal contexts. They can range from simple pro-and-con lists to more complex frameworks involving multiple stages and criteria. Here, we will discuss several established decision-making models and explore how to tailor them to a purpose-driven approach.

The Rational Model is one of the oldest and most straightforward frameworks for decision-making. It involves defining the problem, identifying alternatives, evaluating those alternatives, and then choosing the best option. When tailored to a purpose-driven approach, each step should be filtered through the lens of organizational or individual purpose. For example, when evaluating alternatives, one could weigh options based on how well they align with the defined purpose, ensuring that the chosen solution not only solves the problem but also contributes to fulfilling that purpose.

The Vroom-Yetton-Jago Model focuses on leadership decision-making and emphasizes the level of group involvement. A purpose-driven adaptation could involve consulting team members about how different decisions align with organizational purpose. This inclusive approach could result in more committed and satisfied employees because they see the purpose reflected in the decision-making process.

The OODA Loop (Observe, Orient, Decide, Act) is a decision-making cycle originally formulated for combat operations. It's a continuous feedback loop that can also be tailored for purpose-driven decision-making. In the Observe phase, you could monitor how well the organization or team is aligning with its purpose. During the Orient phase, you could contextualize the information gathered within the framework of that purpose. This purpose-driven orientation will subsequently guide the Decide and Act phases.

The Six Thinking Hats model, developed by Edward de Bono, is another useful tool for purpose-driven decisions. It involves viewing a problem from six different perspectives, each represented by a different colored "hat." When incorporating purpose, an additional "hat" can be added, dedicated solely to considering how each option aligns with the organizational or individual purpose.

Each of these decision-making models can be adapted to incorporate a purpose-driven perspective. The aim is to make decisions that are not only effective in the short-term but also meaningful and impactful in the long-term, aligning actions and choices with broader goals and values.

Challenges and pitfalls in decision-making often occur when quick decisions are required or when there's a lack of information. In many cases, the urge to resolve a problem quickly can result in hasty choices that don't align with an organization's or individual's purpose. One common error is "groupthink," where team members conform to a consensus opinion without critical evaluation of alternatives. This can be detrimental to purpose-driven decision-making, as the most popular choice isn't necessarily the one that best aligns with the overarching goal or mission.

Another frequent mistake is "confirmation bias," where individuals favor information that confirms their existing beliefs. This bias can cloud judgment and lead to decisions that veer off course from the intended purpose. A purpose-focused approach requires open-mindedness and the willingness to consider all available data objectively.

Yet another challenge is "decision fatigue," the declining quality of choices made by an individual after a long session of decision-making. This can be particularly harmful in a purpose-driven context, as it can lead to decisions that are expedient but not necessarily aligned with longer-term goals and values.

To avoid these common pitfalls, it's crucial to embed purpose into the decision-making process at every stage. Start by clearly defining the decision that needs to be made and what purpose it serves. Encourage diverse viewpoints and independent thinking among team members to mitigate the risks of groupthink and confirmation bias. Regularly revisit the organization's mission or individual purpose to make sure the decision aligns with these larger objectives. Take time to step back, especially during long decision-making processes, to avoid decision fatigue and ensure that purpose remains a focal point.

The idea is to be consistently mindful of the purpose at hand and to use it as a yardstick against which all potential choices are measured. By doing so, you're more likely to make decisions that not only solve immediate problems but also contribute to broader goals.

In summary, the role of purpose in decision-making is critical and far-reaching. This chapter dissected the steps involved in the decision-making process, highlighting the importance of weaving purpose into each phase. The significance of ethical considerations was underscored, emphasizing how ethics and purpose should be closely aligned to make meaningful choices. In our discussion about stakeholders, the need to consider multiple interests while staying true to one's mission became evident.

We also delved into real-world case studies that showcased purpose-driven decision-making in action, giving you actionable insights for your journey. We explored various decision-making models that can be tailored to fit a purpose-driven approach. Finally, we looked at the challenges and pitfalls that often occur during decision-making and suggested strategies to mitigate these risks by maintaining alignment with purpose.

As we move on to the next chapter, we will shift our focus to inspiring your team. Building on what you've learned about making purpose-driven decisions, the next section will provide you with techniques to motivate and uplift those you lead. By aligning individual purposes with that of the team and the organization, leaders can create a more committed, effective, and satisfied workforce. The next chapter will equip you with the tools you need to make this alignment a reality, as you continue to lead with purpose.

Exercise 7: Purpose-Driven Decision Matrix

Objective: To practice making decisions that are aligned with your personal or organizational purpose, using a weighted matrix.

Materials Needed:

Pen and paper or a digital spreadsheet

Steps:

1. Identify the Decision: Clearly define the decision you are facing. Write it down at the top of the page or spreadsheet.
2. List Options: Below the decision, list all the possible options you are considering.
3. Identify Criteria: On the side, list the criteria that are important for making this decision. Include 'Alignment with Purpose' as one of the criteria.
4. Weight the Criteria: Assign a weight to each criterion based on its importance. Make sure to give significant weight to 'Alignment with Purpose.' The weights should all add up to 100.
5. Rate Each Option: Rate how well each option fulfills each criterion on a scale of 1 to 10.
6. Calculate: Multiply the rating by the weight for each criterion and sum these up for each option.
7. Analyze: The option with the highest total score is theoretically the best one based on your weighted criteria and alignment with purpose.
8. Reflect: Before finalizing your decision, take some time to reflect. Does the winning option feel right intuitively? Does it align with your ethical considerations? If not, you may need to adjust the weights or reconsider the criteria.

Discussion Questions:

- Was the highest-scoring option surprising to you? Why or why not?
- How did considering 'Alignment with Purpose' impact your decision?
- Are there any ethical considerations that the matrix didn't capture?

By practicing this exercise, you'll get a clearer sense of how to make complex decisions that are in harmony with your larger goals and values. It serves as a practical tool to unify purpose, ethics, and stakeholder interests in your decision-making process.

Chapter 8: Inspiring Your Team

Within the art and science of leadership, inspiring your team stands as one of the most vital components for fostering not only a productive work environment but also a meaningful one. Leaders who successfully inspire their teams unlock a treasure trove of benefits, including increased engagement, higher levels of creativity, and enhanced commitment to organizational goals. The ability to inspire is not just an ancillary skill; it's central to elevating the collective potential of the team and propelling the organization forward.

Purpose can serve as a powerful motivator in this context. When team members understand the 'why' behind their work, they are more likely to invest emotionally and intellectually in their tasks. Purpose acts as a North Star, providing direction and focus, especially during challenging times. It elevates tasks from mere to-dos to a part of a grander mission, making the work personally and collectively significant. Therefore, coupling purpose with leadership strategies can create an environment where inspiration is not sporadic but sustainable. In this chapter, we will delve into how you, as a leader, can tap into the motivating power of purpose to inspire your team consistently and effectively.

Understanding what motivates your team is crucial for effective leadership. Motivation can be broadly classified into two categories: intrinsic and extrinsic. Intrinsic motivation comes from within the individual and is driven by internal rewards like personal satisfaction, curiosity, or the joy of mastering a skill. Extrinsic motivation, on the other hand, is fueled by external factors like salary, bonuses, promotions, or recognition. Both types play a role in shaping employee behavior, but they serve different needs and can be more or less effective depending on the situation.

The role of purpose in motivation is especially significant when considering intrinsic motivation. Purpose can instill a sense of meaning and direction in work, transforming it from a set of tasks to a mission that contributes to a larger goal. This aligns closely with intrinsic motivators, creating a sense of fulfillment and autonomy, as employees feel they are contributing to something greater than themselves. Even in the realm of extrinsic motivation, purpose can add an extra layer of incentive. For instance, bonuses or promotions may be more meaningful when they are seen as a recognition of contributions toward a shared organizational mission rather than just individual achievements.

By comprehending these different types of motivation and recognizing the potent role that purpose can play, leaders are better equipped to craft strategies that resonate with their teams on a deeper level. Not only does this improve performance, but it also fosters a work environment that is more emotionally and intellectually rewarding for everyone involved.

Clear and effective communication is a cornerstone of good leadership, especially when the goal is to inspire a team. But communication is more than just transmitting information; it's also about inspiring action, instilling a sense of purpose, and motivating your team to achieve common goals. Poor communication can lead to misunderstandings, low morale, and decreased productivity, while effective communication can boost team morale, enhance engagement, and improve overall performance.

In the context of inspiring your team, the way you communicate can significantly affect the impact of your message. Articulating the organization's purpose and how each team member contributes to that larger mission can be incredibly motivating. Storytelling is one technique that has proven effective. By framing challenges and successes in the form of stories, leaders can make objectives more relatable and memorable, thus making the team feel more emotionally invested in their work.

Active listening is another key component of inspirational communication. By actively engaging with team members, you show that their opinions are valued, which in turn makes them more receptive to your message. When employees feel heard, they are more likely to contribute ideas and take an active role in problem-solving, thereby becoming more invested in their work.

Feedback is also a vital part of communication. Constructive feedback can help team members understand where they stand and what is expected of them. If given appropriately and effectively, feedback can serve as a motivational tool that can help individuals improve and grow, both professionally and personally.

Leaders can employ rhetorical techniques to make their message more compelling. The use of metaphors, analogies, and even humor can make the message stick and resonate more deeply with the team. Non-verbal cues like body language, eye contact, and tone of voice also play a crucial role in how your message is received.

Effective communication is multifaceted, involving both the content of the message and the way it's delivered. By understanding and applying different techniques tailored to your team's needs and preferences, you can turn communication into a powerful tool for inspiring and motivating your team.

Leadership style plays a critical role in how effectively you can inspire your team. The manner in which you lead not only sets the tone for the organizational culture but also directly impacts employee motivation, job satisfaction, and ultimately, productivity. Two leadership styles often cited for their potential to inspire are Transformational Leadership and Servant Leadership.

Transformational Leadership is rooted in the ability to inspire and motivate team members by creating a vision for the future that is compelling and engaging. Transformational leaders are often charismatic figures who excel at creating a sense of excitement and urgency around organizational objectives. They instill a sense of purpose in their teams by connecting daily tasks and projects to the broader organizational goals. They are also adept at individualized consideration, recognizing the unique abilities and needs of each team member and tailoring their approach accordingly.

Transformational leaders often use their influence to foster a culture of innovation and excellence. They are generally good at recognizing potential in their team members and nurturing it. This can be especially powerful in promoting personal and professional development, thereby increasing job satisfaction and performance. The leader's ability to articulate a vision, combined with their focus on development and mentorship, typically results in high levels of trust and respect from their team.

Servant Leadership, on the other hand, places the emphasis on the leader as a servant to their team. This leadership style is primarily concerned with the well-being and growth of individuals within the organization. Servant leaders are highly attentive to the emotional and developmental needs of their team members and aim to create an environment where everyone feels valued and supported. They often go out of their way to remove barriers that their team may be facing, helping them to perform at their best.

The focus on team well-being often leads to a more inclusive and cohesive work environment. This can result in higher levels of employee engagement and commitment to the organization. Servant leaders typically build strong relationships within their teams, creating a sense of community and mutual respect. Their style often fosters an environment where employees are more willing to contribute their ideas, knowing that their input is valued.

While both Transformational and Servant Leadership styles have their merits, it's worth noting that the most effective leaders often blend aspects of multiple leadership styles, depending on the specific needs of their team and the challenges they face. What ties these leadership styles together, particularly in the context of inspiration, is their focus on the people they lead. Both styles prioritize the needs, development, and well-being of team members, albeit in different ways. When done effectively, these leadership styles can significantly contribute to a motivated, engaged, and inspired team.

There are several other leadership styles that can inspire and motivate teams, each with its own unique set of principles and practices. Below are additional leadership styles that can be highly effective in inspiring a team.

Democratic Leadership

This style is characterized by a collective decision-making process where each team member's input is valued and considered. The democratic leader fosters an environment where open communication is encouraged, and team members feel heard and respected. This collaborative approach often leads to higher levels of job satisfaction, as employees feel a sense of ownership and commitment towards their work. Moreover, leveraging the diverse skills and perspectives of the team often results in more effective problem-solving and innovation.

Coaching Leadership

In this style, the leader acts as a coach or mentor, focusing on the long-term development of their team members. They provide regular feedback and are committed to helping each person achieve their professional goals. A coaching leader often invests time in understanding the unique skills, strengths, and areas of improvement for each team member. This creates a strong sense of trust and encourages employees to develop their abilities, leading to a more competent and confident team.

Charismatic Leadership

Charismatic leaders possess a natural ability to inspire and motivate others through their personality and actions. They often have an emotional impact on their team, fostering a passionate and energetic work environment. While charismatic leaders are exceptionally skilled at driving enthusiasm and commitment, their style can become problematic if they lack the substance or competence to deliver on their promises.

Participative Leadership

This approach involves team members at all levels in the decision-making process, recognizing that each person can provide valuable insights regardless of their position. Participative leaders often seek feedback from their teams and encourage open discussion around tasks and objectives. This fosters a culture of mutual respect and collaboration, where everyone is invested in the success of the project.

Laissez-faire Leadership

While this hands-off approach might not seem immediately inspiring, it can be highly effective in the right context. A Laissez-faire leader gives their team members a lot of freedom, entrusting them to perform their tasks without much interference. This approach can inspire team members who are highly skilled, motivated, and require little supervision, encouraging innovation and individual problem-solving.

Each of these leadership styles offers a different path to achieving the same end goal: an inspired, engaged, and high-performing team. The best leaders are often those who can adapt their style to meet the changing needs of their team and the specific challenges they face. By understanding and incorporating elements from these various leadership styles, you can create a versatile and robust approach to inspiring your team.

Building a culture of inspiration within a team goes beyond individual leadership styles and taps into the collective ethos of the group. It requires the establishment of certain practices, rituals, and traditions that reinforce a sense of purpose, unity, and achievement. These cultural elements can serve as the backbone of an inspired team, creating an environment where everyone feels valued and motivated to contribute their best.

Rituals and traditions can have a profound impact on team cohesion and morale. Something as simple as a weekly team meeting to discuss wins and challenges can serve as a grounding ritual that keeps everyone connected. Other rituals might include team lunches, quarterly off-site retreats, or a regular "innovation day" where team members can work on projects outside their usual scope. These rituals become the fabric of a team's identity, providing stability and a sense of belonging that can be particularly valuable during times of change or stress.

Recognition is a powerful motivator, and a culture that celebrates achievements, big or small, is often more resilient and inspired. Celebrations can take on many forms, from simple shout-outs in team meetings to more formal recognitions like awards or bonuses. Acknowledging milestones, completed projects, or exceptional performance does more than just boost individual egos; it serves as a reminder of the team's collective capabilities and the value of each member's contribution. Moreover, it can set a standard of excellence, inspiring others to achieve similar heights.

Incorporating both team rituals and celebrations of achievements fosters a culture where inspiration is not a one-off event but a continuous process. These practices serve to reinforce the team's collective identity, and the shared values and goals that come with it. Over time, this builds a virtuous cycle: the team's traditions and rituals offer a regular platform for recognizing and celebrating achievements, which in turn feed back into the overall culture of inspiration. Thus, the team becomes more than just a collection of individuals working towards a common goal; it becomes a community of inspired contributors, each adding their unique value to the collective effort.

Examining case studies provides invaluable perspectives on how leaders have successfully inspired their teams, shaping cultures of innovation, loyalty, and high performance. By dissecting these real-world scenarios, we can extract lessons and actionable insights to apply in our own leadership journeys.

One remarkable example is Satya Nadella, CEO of Microsoft. Taking over a giant tech firm that was considered past its prime, Nadella's leadership breathed new life into the company. He transitioned Microsoft's culture from a "know-it-all" environment to a "learn-it-all" atmosphere. Nadella introduced a series of internal changes to foster innovation and agility, including hackathons and regular meetings to discuss growth mindset principles. Employees soon began to display increased levels of motivation and engagement, contributing to the company's resurgence in the tech industry. What can be taken from Nadella's story is the importance of cultivating an adaptive, learning-focused culture, one that encourages intellectual curiosity and the willingness to make mistakes and grow from them.

Another compelling case study revolves around Mary Barra, CEO of General Motors. Facing a slew of challenges including safety issues and stiff competition, Barra placed a strong emphasis on transparency, accountability, and teamwork. Her clear, direct communication style made expectations transparent, which in turn helped align individual and team goals. Barra emphasized the

126

importance of every role within the company and publicly celebrated team achievements, big and small. The outcome was a more resilient company culture, one that could better navigate the challenges it faced. Barra's approach illustrates the power of open communication and the impact of recognizing and valuing the contributions of all team members.

Analyzing these case studies reveals several key lessons. First, successful leaders tailor their approach to the unique needs and cultures of their organizations; a one-size-fits-all style of leadership is unlikely to inspire diverse teams. Second, the focus on continuous learning, as seen in Microsoft's transition, or the emphasis on transparency and acknowledgment, as with General Motors, can serve as a cornerstone for an inspired and engaged workforce. Finally, the importance of recognizing achievements to foster a sense of collective identity and pride cannot be overstated. When team members feel seen, heard, and valued, they are more likely to be inspired to contribute their best work.

Inspiring a team is not without its challenges, and identifying these obstacles is the first step in navigating them effectively. One common hurdle many leaders face is resistance to change. People are naturally inclined to stick to what they know, making any form of change—whether it's a new company vision or a shift in operational procedures—potentially unsettling. Overcoming this resistance requires clear communication that not only outlines the changes but also explains the 'why' behind them. Incorporating storytelling can be an effective tool here; sharing success stories or parables that align with the change can inspire and make the unfamiliar feel more approachable.

Another issue that leaders often encounter is disengagement among team members. Disengaged employees can sap the energy out of a team, affecting overall performance and morale. Tackling this challenge involves diagnosing the root causes of disengagement. It might be a lack of clarity in roles, insufficient challenges, or not seeing a connection between their work and the company's overarching goals. Once identified, strategies such as job redesign, increased responsibilities, or more transparent communication about how each role contributes to the team's and organization's objectives can be employed to reignite engagement.

The presence of interpersonal conflicts within a team can also serve as a significant barrier to inspiration. Conflicts, if not resolved in a timely and effective manner, can escalate and poison the work environment. Leaders can address this by fostering a culture of open dialogue where team members feel safe to voice concerns and disagreements. Mediation and conflict resolution skills are key abilities that leaders should develop to facilitate this process.

Lastly, external factors such as market competition, economic downturns, or global crises can serve as demotivators. During these times, the ability of a leader to maintain team morale becomes crucial. Effective strategies include staying visible and accessible, maintaining transparent communication about the challenges the organization is facing, and collaboratively developing plans to navigate these obstacles. Providing learning and development opportunities even in times of crisis can also help in keeping the team engaged and inspired.

Understanding and addressing these challenges requires a multi-faceted approach. By combining clear communication, active engagement strategies, conflict resolution skills, and a focus on shared goals and values, leaders can pave the way for a more inspired and cohesive team. These strategies not only serve to overcome obstacles but also act as preventive measures, ensuring that challenges are less likely to derail the team's inspiration and productivity in the long run.

Measuring the level of inspiration within a team is crucial for ensuring that your leadership strategies are effective and that the team is moving in the right direction. While inspiration may seem like an intangible quality, there are concrete metrics and methods that can provide insights into the team's motivational levels and overall morale.

One key metric is employee engagement, which can be measured through regular surveys. Questions that target employees' emotional connection to their work, their understanding of the organizational goals, and their willingness to go above and beyond can provide a comprehensive view of the team's morale. Tools such as Gallup's Q12 Employee Engagement Survey or the Utrecht Work Engagement Scale are commonly used for this purpose.

Job satisfaction is another measurable aspect that can serve as an indicator of inspiration. Job satisfaction rates can be gathered through interviews or surveys, where team members can express their views on job roles, working conditions, and workplace relationships. Low scores can act as red flags that demand immediate attention, while consistently high scores could signify an inspired and satisfied team.

Performance metrics can also serve as a measure of inspiration. While high performance doesn't always equate to high inspiration, consistent or increased productivity is often a result of motivated, inspired team members. However, it's important to view performance metrics alongside other measures like job satisfaction and engagement rates to get a full picture.

Regular assessments are essential in measuring inspiration effectively. Inspiration, motivation, and morale are dynamic qualities that can change over time due to various internal and external factors. Regular check-ins, whether through surveys, one-on-one interviews, or team meetings, allow for a timely understanding of the current state of the team's morale. These regular assessments make it possible to identify trends, whether positive or negative, and take appropriate actions to either continue a successful strategy or implement changes where needed.

Regular assessments provide opportunities for leaders to communicate the importance of team inspiration. When team members see that their well-being and motivation are priorities for the organization, it can itself serve as a source of inspiration. The very act of measuring and discussing inspiration can contribute to a culture where people feel valued, heard, and, in turn, more inspired to contribute to the team's success.

By employing these metrics and assessments, leaders can more effectively gauge the level of inspiration within their team and make informed decisions to foster a more motivated, engaged, and high-performing work environment.

In this comprehensive chapter, we have unpacked the multifaceted concept of inspiring a team and how purpose plays a pivotal role in that process. We started by examining the essence of motivation, distinguishing between different types of motivational factors, and underscoring how a clearly articulated purpose can serve as a powerful intrinsic motivator for your team.

From there, we dove into the realm of communication, outlining how effective dialogues can spark inspiration. By being transparent, authentic, and focused, leaders can significantly elevate the team's engagement levels and thus create a ripple effect of inspiration. Different leadership styles, including transformational and servant leadership, were then explored, each offering its own set of tools for inspiring team members.

We also addressed the critical element of establishing a culture that naturally fosters inspiration. Here, we looked at rituals, traditions, and the importance of celebrating achievements both big and small. These can serve as cultural cornerstones that perpetuate a cycle of inspiration within the team.

We also reviewed real-world case studies, each of which provided tangible examples of how leaders have succeeded in inspiring their teams. These cases offer invaluable insights and clearly illustrate the benefits of leading with inspiration.

Next, we touched upon common challenges and obstacles that may arise in the journey to inspire a team. The aim was to equip you with a realistic outlook and actionable strategies to tackle these challenges head-on.

Finally, we discussed the importance of measuring inspiration, advocating for a multi-metric approach that includes employee engagement surveys, job satisfaction rates, and performance metrics. We emphasized the importance of regular assessments to track progress and make necessary adjustments to your inspiration strategies.

As we prepare to delve into the next chapter, we will shift our focus to a topic that naturally extends from leadership and inspiration: how to handle challenges. A true test of any leader's capabilities, managing adversities is often where your team will look to you for direction, making it another arena where purpose-driven leadership can have a profound impact. Be ready to explore techniques and strategies that not only help in navigating through tough times but also in turning challenges into opportunities for growth and learning.

Exercise 8: Purpose-Driven Inspiration Board

Objective: To create a visual representation that encapsulates the team's shared purpose, thereby serving as a source of daily inspiration and motivation.

Materials Needed:

Large poster board or digital equivalent
Magazines, newspapers, printed inspirational quotes (for physical board)
Markers, stickers, glue, scissors (for physical board)

Steps:

1. Set the Context: Brief your team about the importance of having a shared source of inspiration that resonates with the team's purpose. Explain that you'll be creating a collective 'Inspiration Board.'
2. Brainstorm: Have a brainstorming session where each team member can share what inspires them in relation to the team's purpose. This could be quotes, images, or even specific experiences.
3. Collect Material: Team members should gather or create material that can go on the board. For a physical board, this could mean cutting pictures from magazines or writing out quotes. For a digital board, members can find images, videos, or digital quotes.
4. Assemble the Board: In a communal space or during a team meeting, assemble the board with all the gathered materials. If you're working remotely, this can be done on a shared digital platform.
5. Presentation: Once the board is assembled, have a team meeting where it is unveiled. Each team member can explain the reasoning behind their contributions to the board.

Place the physical board in a place where everyone can see it, like a break room or main workspace. If it's digital, make it easily accessible, perhaps as a shared background or accessible via a quick link. Make it a monthly or quarterly ritual to update the board to keep the inspiration fresh and aligned with any evolving aspects of the team's purpose.

Discussion Questions:

- How does this board inspire you to align with the team's purpose?
- What other forms of inspiration could be integrated into our daily routines?
- How can we hold each other accountable for remaining inspired and aligned with our team's purpose?

This exercise not only serves as a constant source of inspiration but also strengthens team cohesion and collective alignment with your purpose.

Chapter 9: Handling Challenges

In leadership, facing challenges is not just a possibility; it's a guarantee. From internal issues like team conflicts or low morale to external pressures like market volatility or stiff competition, obstacles come in various shapes and sizes. Yet, what separates effective leaders from the rest is not the absence of challenges but the ability to navigate them successfully. It's essential to understand that difficulties are par for the course in any leadership journey, a natural part of the growth process for both individuals and organizations.

The role of purpose in navigating these inevitable challenges cannot be overstated. Purpose serves as your compass, providing both direction and motivation when the going gets tough. It's the force that helps you remember why you started on this journey in the first place, guiding your decisions and giving you a sense of clarity amidst the chaos. When challenges arise, as they surely will, a well-defined purpose can serve as a stabilizing factor, helping to keep your team united and focused. Purpose provides not just a sense of what you're working towards but also offers the resilience and motivation required to overcome hurdles. It fills you and your team with the courage to face adversity head-on, armed with the conviction that you're fighting for something meaningful.

So, as we dive into this chapter, keep in mind that challenges are not only unavoidable but also valuable learning experiences. We will explore various types of challenges, strategies for handling them, and how a strong sense of purpose can make all the difference.

In the realm of leadership, challenges can be broadly categorized into two types: external and internal. Let's delve into both to better equip you for the obstacles you may face.

External Challenges

Navigating external challenges requires a leadership approach that is both proactive and reactive. Market shifts, for example, are inevitable, especially in today's fast-paced world where innovation is constant. One day, you might be at the top of your industry, and the next, a disruptive technology could render your business model obsolete. Here, agility is paramount. Your organization needs to be structured in a way that it can pivot swiftly. Yet, agility alone is not enough; your moves must align with your overarching purpose to maintain the integrity and focus of your business.

Competition, another significant external challenge, is a constant in business. Whether you're a startup or an established enterprise, you'll face competition in some form. The challenge lies in differentiating yourself while staying true to your purpose. Competitors can drive you to innovate, but they can also lead you into a reactive posture where you're always playing catch-up. Here, your purpose becomes your strategic anchor, helping you to assess which competitive moves align with your mission and which do not.

Regulatory changes and geopolitical factors further complicate the landscape. A change in policy can force you to recalibrate your operations, and geopolitical instability can impact your supply chain or market access. In these instances, risk mitigation strategies that include diversification and robust compliance programs become crucial. Again, your purpose serves as a guiding principle to evaluate how to adapt without compromising your core values.

Natural disasters and other unforeseen events are external challenges that are least under your control. The COVID-19 pandemic is a recent example that caught many businesses off guard. The resilience to survive such extreme circumstances often comes from a collective sense of purpose that enables teams to rally together and navigate through the crisis.

In sum, external challenges are varied and complex, requiring multifaceted strategies for effective management. While you cannot control these challenges, your reaction to them is within your control. By employing agility, differentiation, risk mitigation, and resilience—all guided by a clear sense of purpose—you can not only navigate these challenges but also turn some of them into opportunities for growth and enhancement.

Internal Challenges

Internal challenges pose a unique set of problems for leaders because they directly influence the human element of an organization. Issues like team conflicts can be especially corrosive because they create rifts in the very fabric that holds the organization together. Addressing these conflicts necessitates strong interpersonal skills and emotional intelligence from leaders. The resolution often involves difficult conversations, mediation, or even restructuring teams. While doing so, the organization's purpose can serve as a framework for mediation. By redirecting the focus to shared goals and core values, conflicts can often be deescalated and resolved more effectively.

Low morale, another frequent internal challenge, has a domino effect on the organization. It decreases productivity, increases turnover, and can even lead to reputational damage if not addressed. Leaders must identify the root causes, which could be anything from work-life balance issues to lack of career growth, and then address them in a way that boosts morale without compromising the organization's objectives. A clear organizational purpose can serve as a rallying point to elevate morale. Employees who understand their role in a larger mission are more likely to be engaged and satisfied in their jobs.

Skill gaps and resource deficiencies are further internal challenges that can be critical but are often solvable. Training programs, mentorship, and even external hires can address skill gaps, while efficient resource allocation and potentially sourcing additional funding can resolve resource deficiencies. Again, aligning these solutions with the organizational purpose ensures that they contribute to long-term goals rather than just serving as short-term fixes.

Ethical dilemmas, perhaps the most complex of internal challenges, require a nuanced and thoughtful approach. Such dilemmas can place you at the crossroads of profitability and doing what's right, creating a tension that's not easily resolvable. A robust ethical framework, stemming from the organization's purpose and values, can provide guidance in these complex situations.

While internal challenges are generally more controllable than external ones, they require a different set of skills and strategies to manage effectively. Strong leadership, grounded in a well-defined purpose, can navigate these challenges by focusing on interpersonal relationships, employee well-being, skill development, resource allocation, and ethical considerations. This approach doesn't just solve immediate problems; it also strengthens the organizational culture and sets the stage for sustainable success.

Both types of challenges demand different approaches for resolution but having a well-defined purpose can greatly assist in handling them effectively. Your purpose can act as a guidepost, helping you and your team make aligned decisions and find creative solutions. Importantly, a clear purpose can also provide the emotional sustenance required to weather these challenges, making the journey not just bearable but also more meaningful.

Leveraging purpose during times of crisis can serve as an organizational North Star, guiding teams and leaders through uncertainty and complexity. When a crisis hits, the initial reaction can often be confusion and disarray. Employees may be unsure about their roles or the best course of action. Leaders might struggle with decision-making due to rapidly changing circumstances. In such a scenario, a clearly articulated and well-understood purpose can offer a sense of direction that is critical for maintaining team cohesion.

Team cohesion is more than just a "nice-to-have" during a crisis; it's an absolute necessity. An organization that is fragmented or disoriented will find it difficult to respond effectively to urgent challenges. The unity formed by a shared purpose facilitates better communication and quicker decision-making because it establishes a common ground that everyone can agree on. Whether it's adapting to a sudden market downturn, shifting to remote work, or dealing with any other crisis, a cohesive team driven by purpose can pivot more efficiently. When employees understand how their actions contribute to larger organizational goals, even in times of crisis, their focus sharpens, and their commitment deepens. It's not just about surviving the crisis; it's about emerging from it stronger and more aligned than before.

Purpose plays an equally crucial role in decision-making during crises. Often, crisis situations present leaders with a series of difficult choices that can have long-lasting impacts. Decisions must be made swiftly, but they also need to be in sync with the organization's core values and long-term vision. Here is where a clearly defined purpose comes in. It acts as a litmus test for evaluating options and making choices that align with the organization's mission. When faced with several paths, asking the simple question, "Does this align with our purpose?" can help eliminate options that might offer a quick fix but could undermine the organization's values. This focus on purpose can also make the decision-making process more transparent and easier to communicate, which in turn builds trust among team members during turbulent times.

A well-articulated organizational purpose can be an invaluable asset in times of crisis. It helps maintain team cohesion by providing a shared goal that keeps everyone aligned. Moreover, it simplifies decision-making by serving as a foundational principle against which all choices can be measured. This dual role of purpose can not only guide an organization safely through a crisis but also position it for greater success and alignment in the post-crisis landscape.

Effective crisis communication is one of the most critical aspects of leadership, especially during trying times. Leaders who can communicate transparently and maintain team morale during crises are better positioned to steer their organization toward stability and, eventually, recovery.

Transparency in communication serves multiple purposes. It builds trust among team members, dispels rumors, and allows everyone to have a shared understanding of the situation. When an issue arises that threatens the organization, vague or misleading information can often lead to speculation and create unnecessary panic. In contrast, clear, accurate, and timely information can help employees understand the challenges ahead and the steps being taken to address them.

Moreover, transparent communication means not just relaying good news or sugarcoating the issues. It also involves sharing bad news, when necessary, but doing so in a way that is both sensitive and constructive. By being open about the challenges faced, leaders can foster an environment of mutual respect and collective problem-solving. Employees are more likely to contribute ideas and be part of the solution when they fully understand the issues at hand. However, transparency doesn't mean oversharing; leaders must strike a balance to ensure that they are providing enough information to keep the team informed without overwhelming them with details that may create more confusion.

While transparent communication provides the framework, maintaining team morale during tough times is the fuel that keeps the organization running. When crises strike, it's easy for employees to become disheartened, which in turn can affect productivity and engagement. Here, the role of purpose becomes crucial. Leaders should continually remind their teams of the organization's overarching goals and how each member contributes to these objectives. Celebrating small wins, even if they seem trivial compared to the challenges faced, can boost spirits and serve as a reminder that progress is being made.

Leaders should consider the emotional well-being of their teams. Simple acts like regular check-ins, acknowledging efforts, and offering words of encouragement can go a long way in maintaining morale. Leaders should be empathetic, approachable, and genuinely concerned for their team members, which will likely inspire a greater sense of commitment and loyalty from the team. These actions may seem small, but their cumulative effect can profoundly impact how well an organization navigates through crises.

Crisis communication that is transparent and focused on maintaining team morale not only helps organizations weather tough times but also strengthens the team's cohesion and commitment to their shared goals. These strategies enable an organization to deal more effectively with challenges, making it more resilient and better prepared for future crises.

Decision-making in a crisis is an intense and often high-stakes endeavor. The challenges of a volatile, uncertain, complex, and ambiguous situation make every choice crucial. Here, two essential aspects come to the fore: a well-thought-out process for decision-making and the anchoring role that purpose can play to guide those decisions.

In terms of process, effective decision-making in a crisis starts with a rapid assessment of the situation. A swift but thorough analysis of the circumstances is essential to understand the scale, impact, and urgency of the crisis. Immediate threats and long-term consequences should both be considered. Leaders should gather input from relevant experts and team members to ensure that all angles are considered. This comprehensive understanding then becomes the foundation upon which decisions are made.

Once the situation is assessed, leaders should evaluate the available options. Here, scenario planning can be invaluable. By thinking through various situations and potential outcomes, leaders can better anticipate the ripple effects of their choices. This also provides an opportunity to assess the risks and benefits associated with each option. Time is often of the essence in a crisis, but hasty decisions without adequate consideration can exacerbate the situation rather than mitigate it. Therefore, a balance between speed and thoroughness is key.

The next step is to actually make the decision and promptly communicate it to the team, along with the rationale behind it. Clear communication, as discussed earlier, is vital during a crisis. After the decision is made and shared, swift implementation is the next course of action. This often involves delegating tasks, mobilizing resources, and perhaps most critically, monitoring the outcomes to make any necessary adjustments.

Incorporating purpose into crisis decisions adds an extra layer of complexity but also offers an invaluable guide. Purpose acts like a compass, providing direction when the way is unclear. It serves as a constant amidst the variables, helping leaders and teams to align their short-term actions with long-term objectives. When faced with tough choices, asking how each option aligns with the organization's core purpose can bring clarity and focus.

For example, if an organization's purpose is to promote sustainability, then in a financial crisis, options that involve cutting corners on environmental responsibilities would likely be off the table. This might make the decision-making process more challenging in the short term but staying true to the organization's purpose can have long-term benefits, such as enhanced brand reputation and employee satisfaction.

Crisis decision-making is a complex, high-stakes process that requires rapid but careful analysis, scenario planning, and execution. The incorporation of an organization's purpose into this process can act as a guiding light, helping to align immediate actions with long-term goals. By adhering to a clear process and staying anchored in purpose, leaders can make decisions that not only navigate the immediate crisis but also position the organization for future success.

Building resilience within a team is not just a short-term tactic for survival but a long-term strategy for thriving, especially in the face of challenges. Resilience is the ability to bounce back from setbacks, adapt to change, and keep going in the face of adversity. It involves not just individual capabilities but also collective strengths, attitudes, and behaviors that make a team more cohesive and robust.

Starting with strategies to build resilience, one of the most effective approaches is promoting a culture of openness and trust. Creating an environment where team members feel comfortable sharing their thoughts, concerns, and even failures can be liberating. It fosters a culture of psychological safety, which is a cornerstone of resilience. When people feel safe, they are more likely to take risks, voice their opinions, and contribute to problem-solving, all of which are crucial during challenging times.

Another key strategy involves resource availability and utilization. This includes not just physical resources such as equipment and financial capital but also intangibles like time, knowledge, and skills. Ensuring that the team has the resources they need and knows how to use them efficiently can boost confidence and enhance resilience.

Training and development programs can also play a significant role. From skills training to emotional intelligence workshops, equipping your team with the tools they need to succeed not only enhances individual capabilities but also contributes to collective resilience. Stress management techniques, mindfulness training, and even physical fitness programs can help team members become more resilient individually and, by extension, contribute to team resilience.

One often overlooked strategy is the celebration of wins, both big and small. Recognizing and celebrating achievements can uplift the team's spirit and provide the motivation to tackle more significant challenges. It serves as a reminder of the team's capabilities and accomplishments, reinforcing a collective sense of efficacy.

Regarding the benefits of a resilient team, the immediate advantage is the enhanced ability to handle challenges effectively. A resilient team is better equipped to navigate crises, make robust decisions, and come up with innovative solutions. They are more adaptable to change, which is particularly crucial in today's fast-paced business environment.

Resilience often leads to improved well-being among team members. Lower levels of stress, higher job satisfaction, and improved physical and emotional health are some of the positive outcomes. This not only benefits the individuals but also contributes to lower turnover rates, less absenteeism, and higher productivity, providing a competitive edge to the organization.

Resilience fosters a more positive and proactive work culture. A resilient team is more likely to take the initiative, show commitment, and exhibit leadership qualities, which can be infectious and contribute to a virtuous cycle of resilience throughout the organization.

Building a resilient team involves multiple strategic steps, including fostering a culture of trust, ensuring resource availability, investing in training, and celebrating achievements. The benefits are manifold, impacting not only the team's ability to handle challenges but also contributing to individual well-being and organizational success. By investing in resilience, leaders can prepare their teams for not just surviving but thriving in the face of any challenge.

Navigating a crisis is fraught with potential missteps, and even seasoned leaders can make mistakes when under extreme pressure. It's crucial to understand common pitfalls to steer clear of them and handle challenges more effectively.

One frequent mistake during crises is acting impulsively rather than thoughtfully. Leaders may feel pressured to make quick decisions to demonstrate control over the situation. However, these hastily made decisions can be poorly thought out and may exacerbate the problem rather than solve it. The best course of action is to slow down, gather all available information, consult with experts if possible, and then make a calculated decision.

Another issue is poor communication. In crisis situations, the rumor mill can spin out of control, causing panic among team members. Leaders might withhold information to prevent panic or avoid appearing uncertain, but this often has the opposite effect. A lack of clear, transparent communication can fuel anxiety and mistrust. It's crucial to keep lines of communication open, update your team regularly, and admit when you don't have all the answers. The goal is to provide honest, clear information to maintain trust and prevent misinformation from spreading.

Failure to prioritize is also common during crises. When everything seems urgent, there's a risk of spreading resources too thin, trying to solve all problems at once. However, not all issues have the same level of importance or urgency. Leaders need to assess the situation and determine what requires immediate attention and what can wait. Resource allocation should align with these priorities to tackle the most critical issues first.

Leaders may also fall into the trap of isolating themselves to solve problems, viewing leadership as a solo endeavor. This approach not only places an undue burden on the leader but also deprives the team of the opportunity to contribute. It's vital to remember that a crisis is a collective challenge requiring a collective response. Encouraging input from team members can bring in diverse perspectives and might offer solutions that one person couldn't see alone.

Lastly, a failure to adapt can be disastrous in a crisis situation. Leaders might hold onto tried-and-true methods or previously successful strategies, even when they're not applicable to the current challenge. Being flexible and willing to adapt is crucial when navigating uncharted waters. Leaders must be open to changing course when circumstances evolve or when it becomes clear that the current strategy isn't working.

Avoiding these pitfalls involves a combination of self-awareness, careful planning, and effective communication. Keep in mind that every crisis is a learning opportunity. Even if you make mistakes, the key is to recognize them quickly, adapt, and prevent them from occurring again in the future. A crisis is often a litmus test for leadership, and by avoiding these common mistakes, you can lead your team more effectively through the challenges that inevitably arise.

As we reach the end of this chapter on handling challenges, let's take a moment to recap some of the fundamental strategies that can make a significant difference in crisis management. We've explored the types of challenges you might face, both external and internal, and the necessity of understanding the unique aspects of each. We've also discussed the importance of a clearly defined organizational purpose during a crisis, as it serves as a guidepost for making tough decisions and unifying the team. Communication emerged as another cornerstone, especially transparent and frequent updates to maintain trust and morale among team members.

Effective decision-making in a crisis often involves gathering comprehensive information, consulting with experts or team members, and taking a calculated approach rather than acting impulsively. The role of purpose should not be overlooked here; it can serve as a guiding light in uncertain times, helping to align decisions with core values and long-term goals. We also delved into the necessity of building a resilient team, which involves not only strategies for coping with current challenges but also preparing for future ones. And, of course, we covered some of the most common pitfalls in crisis management, offering advice on how to avoid these mistakes to navigate challenges more successfully.

Having examined these various aspects of crisis management, you're better equipped to face the challenges that inevitably arise in leadership. But managing crises is just one part of leading a purpose-driven team. In the next chapter, we'll switch gears to focus on the long-term sustainability of purpose-driven teams. We will explore how to keep the momentum going once you've navigated through the immediate challenges, ensuring that your team remains aligned with its purpose in the long run. The strategies we will discuss aim not just for survival but for ongoing growth and success.

Exercise 9: Purpose-Driven Crisis Simulation

Objective: To simulate a challenging scenario that tests the team's alignment with its purpose, thereby preparing team members for real-life crises and reinforcing the importance of sticking to the team's purpose during trying times.

Materials Needed:

Scenario scripts or descriptions
A timer
Recording devices (optional, for review)

Steps:

1. Introduction: Begin by reminding the team of its shared purpose. Discuss how challenges and crises can either derail a team or make it stronger, depending on how well the team holds to its purpose.
2. Divide and Brief: Divide the team into smaller groups and give each a crisis scenario related to your industry or business. The scenario should be challenging enough to push the team members to consider diverging from their purpose.
3. Scenario Execution: Each group has a set amount of time to discuss and decide how to handle the crisis, keeping the team's purpose in mind. A recorder or a scribe should keep notes on the decision-making process.
4. Time's Up: When time is up, each group must present their decisions to the rest of the team, focusing on how they aligned their choices with the team's purpose.
5. Debrief: The team collectively discusses each group's choices, focusing on the alignment with the team's purpose. This is also a chance to discuss what was difficult about making purpose-aligned choices under pressure.
6. Review and Reflect: If the sessions were recorded, review them to examine body language, tone, and other non-verbal

cues. Discuss what these reveal about alignment and commitment to purpose under pressure.

7. Consolidate Learning: Summarize the key takeaways from the exercise, reinforcing how the team's shared purpose can guide them through real-life challenges.

Discussion Questions:

- Was it difficult to stick to our purpose during a crisis? Why or why not?
- Were there any moments where team members wanted to diverge from the team's purpose? What made you reconsider?
- How can we improve our crisis-handling while staying true to our purpose?

This exercise will not only give your team practical experience in handling crises but also solidify the importance of your team's purpose as a guiding force during challenging times.

Part IV: Sustainable Purpose

As we venture into Part IV of this comprehensive exploration on purpose-driven leadership, we arrive at a pivotal juncture: sustainability. The chapters preceding this section have armed you with the knowledge, strategies, and practical insights necessary to instill a sense of purpose in yourself, your team, and your entire organization. You've learned how to align personal and organizational goals, inspire your team, and navigate the challenges that inevitably crop up in any leadership journey. While these are essential skills and perspectives, they form just part of the equation. Now, we pivot to consider the long haul. How do we maintain the integrity and effectiveness of a purpose-driven approach over time?

Sustainability in this context doesn't merely pertain to longevity but to a form of enduring relevance. A purpose that cannot stand the test of time will ultimately weaken, losing its inspirational power and its capacity to guide decision-making. But a truly sustainable purpose evolves while staying rooted in core principles. It adapts to new challenges, grows with the team, and provides a steady focal point amid change. In the chapters that follow, we will delve into the critical aspects of sustainable purpose, turning our attention to topics often relegated to the periphery of leadership discussions but are, in fact, central to long-term success.

In Chapter 10, "Measuring the Impact," we will discuss the key performance indicators and metrics that can help you evaluate the effectiveness of your purpose-driven initiatives. While purpose is often seen as a qualitative factor, its impact can and should be quantified to ensure that it is serving its intended role effectively. Chapter 11, "Evolving Your Purpose," will tackle the crucial yet often overlooked topic of when and how to reevaluate your purpose. A static purpose is unlikely to serve a dynamic organization, so knowing when to evolve is vital for sustainability.

As we move through this final part of the book, you will gain the tools necessary to keep your purpose relevant and inspiring, not just for a quarter or a fiscal year, but for the lifetime of your organization. Welcome to the journey toward Sustainable Purpose.

Chapter 10: Measuring the Impact

In the realm of purpose-driven organizations, intention and action are only parts of the equation. The third critical component is measurement—evaluating the true impact of your initiatives to know if you're successfully fulfilling your purpose. While the heart and soul of your organization may lie in its mission, its health and effectiveness are gauged by Key Performance Indicators (KPIs) and other metrics. These not only show you where you stand but also illuminate the path forward.

This chapter will delve deep into the indispensable role of KPIs and other evaluation metrics in quantifying the success of your purpose-driven activities. We'll explore how to set meaningful KPIs, the methods to track them, and the tools for interpreting the data. By the end of this chapter, you'll understand the intricacies of measuring the impact and be equipped to make data-driven decisions for the future. So, let's embark on this analytical yet essential aspect of leading with purpose.

Key Performance Indicators, or KPIs, serve as vital signposts on the journey of any purpose-driven organization. They are quantifiable metrics that help leaders and teams gauge how well the organization is performing in relation to its mission and objectives. But these aren't just arbitrary numbers; they are carefully chosen to reflect the most important activities and outputs, acting as a compass that directs you toward your purpose. Understanding KPIs, therefore, is not just a task for the analytical department or a line item on a manager's to-do list; it's a fundamental practice that informs strategic decision-making at every level of the organization.

In a purpose-driven context, KPIs go beyond traditional financial metrics like revenue, profit margins, and shareholder returns. They encompass a broader range of indicators that capture social impact, employee engagement, customer satisfaction, and environmental responsibility, among others. For example, an organization focused on sustainability might track metrics related to carbon footprint reduction or waste management effectiveness. Those committed to social justice may monitor diversity and inclusion statistics or community outreach impact. Employee engagement scores, customer lifetime value, and net promoter scores are other common KPIs that offer insights into the internal and external effectiveness of an organization's purpose.

As the landscape in which your organization operates changes, so too will the metrics that are most relevant to understanding your impact. The first step is knowing what to measure, and from there, how to interpret the data in a way that can drive meaningful change. By understanding and implementing KPIs effectively, you lay down the tracks for your organization's journey toward fulfilling its purpose. These metrics offer a tangible way to translate lofty ideals and broad objectives into measurable outcomes. Through real-world examples and actionable insights, this chapter will make the abstract concrete, guiding you in the intricate task of aligning your KPIs with your overarching organizational purpose.

Quantifying qualitative aspects is an exercise in the delicate balance between the measurable and the intangible. When dealing with elements such as employee satisfaction, community impact, or societal change, the metrics can be elusive, but they are not impossible to capture. It's crucial to remember that not everything that counts can be counted, and not everything that can be counted counts. However, in the organizational context, turning these qualitative aspects into quantifiable metrics helps to create a more holistic picture of success aligned with your purpose.

Starting with employee engagement and satisfaction, traditional methods often used are surveys and questionnaires that capture sentiments on job satisfaction, work-life balance, and the perceived value of the work being done. Advanced tools are also emerging, which use analytics to measure real-time engagement through various metrics, such as the frequency and type of employee interactions within a digital workspace. While these tools can provide valuable quantitative data, it's essential to view them in conjunction with qualitative feedback from one-on-ones, team meetings, and other forums where employees express their views and emotions more openly.

Similarly, when it comes to measuring your impact on the community or broader society, metrics can range from the straightforward—like the number of volunteer hours logged by employees or dollars donated to charitable causes—to more nuanced measures like social return on investment (SROI). SROI attempts to quantify social impact in monetary terms, evaluating the broader social and environmental value generated by every dollar spent. More specific metrics might also include indicators such as the number of people reached through educational programs, health outcomes from community clinics, or access to clean water in underserved communities.

The key in quantifying these qualitative aspects lies in choosing metrics that resonate most strongly with your organizational purpose and that are actionable. These metrics should inform and guide strategy, not just serve as a retrospective scorecard. Hence, aligning these soft metrics with hard business objectives is vital for a comprehensive approach to fulfilling your organizational mission.

Through real-world examples and actionable insights, this chapter aims to guide you in identifying, tracking, and interpreting these qualitative aspects in a way that aligns with your organization's larger purpose and goals. By effectively quantifying these softer aspects of business, you provide a more rounded view of how closely your operations align with your purpose and what you may need to adjust to stay on the path of impactful work.

The process of data collection is foundational to measuring the impact of a purpose-driven organization. How you collect data can significantly affect the quality of insights you gain, which in turn informs your strategies and actions. In this context, it's imperative to discuss the various tools available for data collection as well as the optimal frequency and timing for gathering this data.

Starting with tools, there is an extensive array of options available for gathering different kinds of metrics. Surveys and questionnaires continue to be popular for collecting subjective data such as employee and customer satisfaction. Digital analytics platforms are indispensable for tracking online engagement and customer behavior. Specialized software exists for virtually every kind of metric you might need—whether it's an employee performance management system that tracks individual and team productivity or a customer relationship management system that offers insights into customer interactions and preferences.

However, technological advancements have led to more sophisticated tools that offer real-time analytics and even predictive capabilities. Artificial Intelligence and machine learning algorithms can sift through large sets of data to identify trends or patterns that might not be apparent through manual analysis. Such tools are especially useful in capturing dynamic metrics that change frequently and require quick action. Even for community impact measures, Geographic Information Systems (GIS) can plot the geographic spread and effectiveness of various initiatives, helping to visualize where efforts are making the most impact and where more work is needed.

Once you've chosen the most suitable tools for your specific needs, you'll also need to determine how often this data should be collected. The frequency and timing of data collection are contingent on various factors, including the type of data, the speed at which it changes, and the overall goals of your initiative. For static metrics like annual revenue or customer retention rates, yearly or quarterly assessments may suffice. However, more dynamic metrics like employee engagement or real-time customer satisfaction might require monthly, weekly, or even daily checks.

What's essential is that the frequency of data collection aligns with your organizational objectives and provides actionable insights. Too much data can be as problematic as too little if it leads to information overload and analysis paralysis. Similarly, data collected too infrequently may miss important trends or changes, hindering timely action. Therefore, carefully consider your goals and resources when planning the frequency and timing of data collection.

By employing a thoughtful approach to the tools, you use and the timing of your data collection efforts, you can significantly enhance the effectiveness of your measurement systems. These systems, in turn, can offer valuable insights into how well your organization is aligning with its overarching purpose, and what can be fine-tuned to create even more significant impact.

Interpreting the data, you've gathered is a crucial part of the measurement process. Simply having raw numbers doesn't do much good unless you can turn them into actionable insights that help your organization align more closely with its purpose. In this context, analyzing Key Performance Indicator (KPI) results and making meaningful inferences are two key elements that require considerable attention and expertise.

Analyzing KPI results begins with a clear understanding of what these metrics represent and how they align with your organizational objectives. For instance, if one of your KPIs is employee engagement, a low score could signify a multitude of issues, such as poor work-life balance, lack of career growth opportunities, or a disconnection with the organization's purpose. It's essential to break down each KPI into its constituent parts and understand the variables affecting it. Utilize statistical tools, historical comparisons, and cross-referencing with other KPIs to gain a more nuanced understanding.

Even the most straightforward KPIs can have multiple layers. For example, if customer satisfaction scores have declined, it's insufficient to merely note the dip. The reasons could range from product quality issues to poor customer service. Breaking down this KPI by various demographics or correlating it with specific events or changes in your organization, can offer more detailed insights. Was there a recent change in your product line or service delivery? Did the drop coincide with the departure of a key team member? Investigating these correlations can provide a roadmap for improvement.

Moving on to making meaningful inferences, this is where your analytical work comes to fruition. The objective here is not just to know what the numbers are, but what they mean for your organization. This involves not only scrutinizing the data for trends and patterns but also interpreting its broader implications. For example, if you've found that employee engagement is highest among teams that are most aligned with your organization's purpose, the inference could be that instilling a sense of purpose can boost productivity and job satisfaction. These insights should serve as a catalyst for action, directing you to areas where adjustments or interventions are needed.

Inferences should also be checked for validity and relevance. It's easy to jump to conclusions based on a narrow set of data or personal biases. Engage multiple stakeholders in the interpretation process, seek external validation where possible, and consider conducting pilot tests to confirm your inferences before rolling out broader organizational changes.

The interpretation of your data serves as the connecting bridge between raw numbers and tangible actions. The process involves a rigorous analysis of KPI results to break them down into understandable components, followed by drawing inferences that are both meaningful and actionable. This dual focus ensures that you're not just collecting data for the sake of data but using it as a powerful tool for fulfilling your organization's purpose.

Adjustments and Future Planning are indispensable steps that naturally follow the measurement and interpretation of your Key Performance Indicators (KPIs). Once you've collected the necessary data, analyzed the metrics, and drawn meaningful inferences, the next crucial phase is translating these insights into real-world actions and future strategies. This part of the process is where the rubber meets the road, where you actually start seeing the fruits of your labor in enhancing your organization's alignment with its purpose.

Using data for action planning involves converting your insights into specific, actionable plans that target the areas identified as needing improvement or scaling. For instance, if the data shows a marked decline in customer satisfaction, the action plan could include steps like revising customer service protocols, offering additional training for frontline staff, or even re-evaluating the product or service features. The objective here is to create a set of concrete steps, complete with timelines, responsible parties, and required resources, aimed directly at the issues at hand.

Each action plan should also include a mechanism for monitoring progress. Whether it's regular check-ins with responsible team members or periodic reviews of new data, tracking how well your plan is working is essential for understanding its efficacy. This step ensures that you're not just making changes for the sake of making changes but that those changes are effectively steering your organization closer to its purpose.

Adapting strategies based on metrics is another integral component of this phase. KPIs are not static; they change as your organization evolves and as the external environment shifts. A strategy that worked exceptionally well a year ago may no longer be effective today. This adaptive capacity is especially critical for organizations committed to a dynamic, evolving purpose. It means not only having the flexibility to change but having the systems in place to know when change is necessary.

For instance, if quarterly reviews show that employee engagement is not as robust as it once was, despite various interventions, it might be time to revisit your strategies. Could the engagement programs be out of sync with what your employees currently value? Are there new challenges that the previous strategies had not considered? Adaptation could involve refining existing methods, but it could also mean overhauling approaches that are no longer effective.

The process of adjustments and future planning is essential for bringing your measurement activities full circle. By using your KPI data for action planning and strategy adaptation, you ensure that your organization doesn't just gather data but uses it as a strategic asset. This ongoing cycle of measurement, analysis, action, and adaptation serves to keep your organization not only aligned with its current purpose but also capable of evolving along with that purpose over time.

In the world of purpose-driven organizations, the importance of Key Performance Indicators (KPIs) cannot be overstated. Case studies provide invaluable insights into how other organizations have successfully utilized KPIs to align their operations with their purpose and achieve remarkable results. This section will delve into such examples, offering not just a glimpse into what has worked well but also unearthing the lessons and best practices that can be adopted by others.

One compelling example is that of a healthcare nonprofit organization focused on providing quality healthcare services in underserved communities. They employed KPIs like patient satisfaction scores, the number of healthcare interventions delivered, and community health statistics to gauge their effectiveness. The organization took it a step further by correlating these KPIs with their purpose—improving health outcomes in underserved areas. As a result, they were able to shift resources to community education, thereby increasing awareness about preventive healthcare and achieving a significant decrease in emergency room visits. The lesson here is the value of using KPIs not just as metrics but as tools for strategic decision-making that directly aligns with organizational purpose.

Another example comes from the corporate sector, specifically a technology company committed to sustainability. They set KPIs around the reduction of carbon footprint, use of renewable energy, and employee participation in their sustainability programs. But what stands out is how they used these KPIs to inform their business strategy. By consistently monitoring their carbon footprint data, they opted to invest in more energy-efficient data centers, a move that not only advanced their purpose but also resulted in considerable cost savings. This case teaches us the power of aligning business goals with purpose driven KPIs and illustrates that doing good can also be good for business.

Both these examples illustrate the concept of "double bottom line" accounting, where organizations measure success not just by traditional financial metrics but also by their impact on communities and the environment. Best practices in this realm include the importance of setting clear, measurable KPIs that are directly tied to the organization's purpose; the need for regular data collection and analysis; and the value of using this data to inform both immediate action plans and long-term strategic direction.

Through these case studies, we can see that KPIs are not merely a set of numbers to track performance. When used effectively, they become strategic assets that enable organizations to make informed decisions, adapt to challenges, and ultimately bring their purpose to life. The lessons gleaned offer a roadmap for how to navigate the complexities of aligning everyday operations with broader purpose-driven goals.

In this chapter, we've explored the multifaceted realm of measuring impact within purpose-driven organizations. We started by delving into what Key Performance Indicators (KPIs) are and why they are pivotal for an organization's success. These KPIs serve as more than just metrics; they're the lifelines that connect day-to-day operations with an organization's overarching purpose. We also looked at the challenge of quantifying qualitative aspects, like employee engagement and societal impact, to ensure a more holistic approach to measuring success.

Equally critical is the process of data collection and analysis. We examined the variety of tools available for gathering data and the optimal frequency for such activities. But it's not enough to collect data; organizations must also interpret it effectively to make meaningful inferences. The importance of this was made clear as we discussed how these insights form the basis for future planning and strategic adjustments. Lastly, we drew from real-world case studies to understand how organizations have successfully harnessed the power of KPIs to realize their purpose.

As we move to the next chapter, our focus will shift to the concept of 'Evolving Your Purpose.' Purpose isn't a static concept; it's dynamic, capable of evolving as organizations grow and as societal needs change. A clear set of KPIs and a robust system for measuring impact will be essential tools as you engage in this evolutionary process. We'll examine when and how to reassess your purpose, how to keep it relevant, and how to ensure that it continues to inspire and guide your organization toward meaningful impact. The aim is to equip you with the knowledge and tools you need to make your purpose not just inspiring but also sustainable over the long term.

Exercise 10: Conducting a KPI Audit for Your Purpose-Driven Organization

Objective: To identify, evaluate, and refine the Key Performance Indicators (KPIs) that are most aligned with your organization's purpose. This exercise will also help you understand how to collect and interpret data for these KPIs.

Materials Needed
Whiteboard or large paper sheets
Markers
Laptop or tablet for research

Instructions

1. Identify Current KPIs: Begin by listing all the KPIs currently being tracked in your organization. If your organization is not currently using KPIs, brainstorm some KPIs that you think could be relevant.
2. Categorize the KPIs: Divide these KPIs into categories such as 'Financial,' 'Customer,' 'Employee,' and 'Community/Societal.'
3. Evaluate Relevance: Discuss with your team how each KPI aligns with the organization's purpose. Use a scale of 1-5, where 1 is not aligned and 5 is highly aligned.
4. Research: Take some time to research industry-specific KPIs that are commonly used in purpose-driven organizations. Note down any that you find particularly relevant.
5. Add New KPIs: From your research, add any new KPIs to your list that you feel are more aligned with your purpose.
6. Prioritize: With your updated list, prioritize the KPIs based on their alignment with your purpose and their ease of measurement. Limit yourself to a maximum of 10 KPIs to focus on.
7. Data Collection Methods: For each chosen KPI, discuss and note down the most effective methods for data collection.

8. Action Plans: Finally, for each KPI, brainstorm potential action plans for improvement based on hypothetical low or high performance.
9. Review: Summarize your findings and create a schedule to regularly review these KPIs. This can be monthly, quarterly, or annually depending on the KPI.

Discussion Questions

- How did the exercise help you think differently about measuring impact?
- Were there any KPIs that you found were not aligned with your organization's purpose?
- How will the refined set of KPIs help your organization better achieve its purpose?

This exercise will not only help you align your KPIs with your organizational purpose but will also set the stage for more effective and purposeful decision-making.

Chapter 11: Evolving Your Purpose

Purpose is not a static concept. While the core values and mission of an organization may remain steady over time, the specific purpose that drives you and your team can and should evolve. This adaptability is especially crucial in a world that is constantly changing—economically, socially, and technologically. The alignment of your purpose with both internal and external environments is vital for the ongoing success and relevance of your organization.

In this chapter, we will delve into the nuanced journey of evolving your purpose. We'll explore various factors that could necessitate a reevaluation of your purpose, from shifts in leadership to dramatic market changes. Additionally, we will provide a structured approach to auditing your existing purpose and gathering insights for its possible recalibration.

So, if you're wondering whether your current purpose has lost its resonance or needs fine-tuning, you're in the right place. This chapter aims to be a comprehensive guide for when and how to reevaluate your purpose, offering practical steps, tools, and real-world examples. Through this process, you will not only refine your purpose but also revitalize your team and organizational strategy.

The idea that a purpose statement has a certain lifespan may seem counterintuitive, especially if the statement feels like an authentic reflection of your team's or organization's core mission. However, various factors can contribute to a purpose statement's longevity, or lack thereof, requiring you to consider revisions.

First, let's talk about what makes a purpose statement durable. A well-crafted purpose statement is generally adaptable to different circumstances and can guide your organization through multiple phases of its lifecycle. If your statement is rooted in timeless values and broad enough to encompass a variety of activities and goals, it's more likely to have staying power.

But what are some signs that indicate a need for revisiting your purpose statement? One obvious indicator is when the statement becomes irrelevant to the work you're currently doing. As organizations grow and evolve, they may diversify their offerings or change directions in a way that makes the original purpose too narrow or obsolete.

Another red flag is a noticeable decline in team morale or engagement. If your purpose no longer resonates with your team, it's often a sign that the statement needs refreshing. This could be especially true if there's been a significant change in your workforce, whether through high turnover rates, a merger, or even a generational shift that brings in younger team members with different expectations and values.

A purpose statement isn't set in stone; rather, it should evolve to reflect the current state and aspirations of your organization. Recognizing the factors that contribute to its longevity and being vigilant for signs of obsolescence are critical steps in maintaining a relevant and inspiring purpose.

Revisiting and possibly revising your purpose statement isn't an arbitrary process; certain triggers often signal the need for a reevaluation. These triggers can be both internal and external to the organization.

When we talk about internal changes compelling a reevaluation of a purpose statement, we are looking at alterations within the organizational structure that can significantly affect the company's direction and values. Let's delve into some of these key internal changes in greater detail.

When a new CEO or executive team takes the helm, they bring with them new perspectives, experiences, and possibly a different set of core values. This could lead to a shift in the organization's strategic objectives and even its cultural fabric. A new leader might prioritize innovation over tradition, sustainability over quick profits, or community outreach over aggressive expansion. These shifts often necessitate a reevaluation and potential revision of the purpose statement to ensure it aligns with new leadership visions.

Organizational transformations like mergers, acquisitions, or internal restructuring often necessitate a revisit of the purpose statement. In the case of a merger or acquisition, two different organizational cultures and purposes must harmonize into a cohesive new entity. Existing purpose statements may no longer be applicable, or at the least, they may need to be adjusted to reflect the ethos and objectives of the newly formed organization.

Sometimes the organization itself undergoes an evolution in what it does best. For example, a tech company might transition from hardware to software; a retailer might pivot from physical stores to e-commerce. These shifts in core competencies require an updated purpose statement that reflects the company's new focal points. Similarly, a significant change in employee demographics—like a younger workforce joining the company or increased diversity—could call for a revised purpose statement that is more in tune with the values and expectations of the new demographic mix.

Understanding these internal changes and their implications is essential for keeping your purpose statement aligned with the current state and future direction of your organization.

External factors play a crucial role in shaping the relevance and applicability of your organization's purpose statement. These external elements often come in the form of market dynamics, technological revolutions, legislative changes, or shifts in societal values. Here's a deeper look into how these factors can impact your purpose statement.

Markets are not static; they evolve, sometimes rapidly. Whether it's due to an economic downturn, a change in consumer preferences, or disruptions caused by innovations, market shifts can make your existing purpose statement seem out of touch or irrelevant. For instance, if you are in the business of manufacturing DVDs and the world has moved on to streaming services, sticking to a purpose statement centered around 'providing the best physical media' might require rethinking.

With the pace of technological change accelerating, it's possible for an organization to find its purpose statement becoming obsolete. Advances in artificial intelligence, blockchain, or clean energy, for example, can create new opportunities and challenges that were not envisioned when the original purpose statement was crafted. Adapting to these technological shifts often involves revising your purpose to incorporate new realms of possibilities.

New laws or regulations can have a substantial impact on your business operations and, by extension, your purpose statement. For instance, stricter environmental regulations might compel an energy company to revise its purpose statement to reflect a greater commitment to sustainability. Changes in trade laws, data protection statutes, or employment regulations could similarly trigger a need to revisit your organizational purpose.

In today's world, businesses are increasingly expected to play a role in addressing societal issues, whether it's sustainability, social justice, or community development. A heightened focus on such matters can make an existing purpose statement feel outdated or inadequate. If societal priorities have shifted towards issues that your current purpose does not address, it might be time to align your purpose statement more closely with these emerging societal values.

Being attuned to these external factors is essential for maintaining a purpose statement that is both relevant and resonant. A proactive approach to reevaluating your purpose in the face of these changes ensures that your organization remains aligned with the broader context in which it operates.

Both internal changes and external factors are significant triggers that could indicate the need for revising your purpose statement. Being attuned to these changes and understanding their potential impact on your organization is crucial for maintaining a relevant and compelling purpose.

The process of reevaluating an organizational purpose is not to be taken lightly. It involves a series of well-considered steps that ensure the newly revised purpose is aligned with both internal realities and external conditions. The following are some key steps to consider in the process of purpose reevaluation:

The first step in this journey is a thorough audit of the existing purpose statement. Begin by examining how well it has served the organization thus far. Assess its relevancy, clarity, and alignment with the company's current state and objectives. Review key performance indicators and other metrics to see if the organization has been successful in living up to its stated purpose. This audit should also include an analysis of any disconnects between the current purpose and the prevailing conditions, either within the company or in the external environment. A purpose statement that has been effective in guiding organizational decisions and actions is more likely to need minor tweaking rather than a complete overhaul.

No purpose statement exists in isolation; it has implications for a range of stakeholders, from employees and customers to investors and even the broader community. As such, gathering insights from these stakeholders can provide invaluable perspectives. Utilize surveys, focus groups, and one-on-one interviews to collect feedback on the existing purpose statement.

Employees can offer insights into how the purpose affects organizational culture and daily operations. Customers can shed light on whether your purpose aligns with their values and needs, thus impacting their loyalty and engagement. Investors can provide a viewpoint on how well the purpose serves the long-term strategy and financial health of the company.

These steps form the backbone of the reevaluation process. They are essential in identifying whether the existing purpose statement still serves the organization well or needs a revamp to align better with current realities. The insights derived from these steps will serve as a foundation for any adjustments or rewriting that may be necessary, ensuring that the new purpose statement is both meaningful and effective.

Involving your team in the process of reevaluating the organizational purpose is crucial for several reasons. One of the most effective ways to gather team input is by creating open channels of communication where employees can freely express their opinions and thoughts. This could be facilitated through town hall meetings, anonymous surveys, or even informal group discussions. These methods provide team members with a platform to voice their concerns, suggestions, or affirmations about the current purpose and any proposed changes.

But why is this collective buy-in so important? First, employees are more likely to be engaged and motivated when they feel a sense of ownership over the organizational purpose. Their buy-in ensures that the purpose is not just a top-down directive but a collective vision that everyone is committed to. Second, team members often have unique insights into various aspects of the business, from customer interaction to daily operations, which can be invaluable when reevaluating the purpose. Their perspectives can provide a more rounded view, ensuring that the revised purpose is both practical and aspirational.

Therefore, the process of reevaluating an organizational purpose should be as inclusive as possible to ensure it accurately reflects the collective will and wisdom of the entire team. This not only enhances the quality and depth of the revised purpose but also fosters a sense of community and shared responsibility among team members.

Surveys and questionnaires are often the go-to tools for collecting quantitative data from a large number of participants. These instruments can be administered online or in-person and can contain a mix of multiple-choice, Likert scale, and open-ended questions. Surveys are particularly useful for gathering general opinions and can be analyzed statistically to identify trends, patterns, or areas of concern.

On the other hand, interviews and focus groups provide a more qualitative approach, allowing for a deeper exploration of attitudes, perceptions, and beliefs. Interviews are usually one-on-one and offer the opportunity to delve into nuanced aspects of individual experiences and opinions. Focus groups, meanwhile, bring together a diverse cross-section of team members to discuss various topics in a structured setting. The interaction among participants can yield valuable insights and even highlight areas of consensus or contention that may not be evident through surveys.

Both sets of tools—surveys and questionnaires, interviews and focus groups—have their strengths and weaknesses. Surveys are efficient for collecting data from a large group but may not capture the full context or complexities of individual opinions. Interviews and focus groups, while rich in detail, can be time-consuming and may not be feasible for gathering opinions from everyone in a large organization.

Using a combination of these methods can offer a more comprehensive picture, ensuring that the reevaluated purpose is grounded in both broad trends and individual experiences. This multi-faceted approach to data gathering is often the most effective way to ensure that the evolving purpose remains aligned with the needs, expectations, and values of all stakeholders.

Several noteworthy examples of organizations successfully evolving their purpose statements can offer guidance and inspiration. Take the case of a tech company that initially focused solely on consumer electronics but later expanded into providing comprehensive digital ecosystems, including software and services. The company's original purpose statement, focused on "making great products," was broadened to encompass "enriching people's lives through technology." This new purpose aligned with the company's evolved identity and diversified product range, reinforcing a broader mission that still resonated with the original core values.

Another instance involves a nonprofit originally dedicated to local community development that grew its scope to include international projects. The organization's purpose evolved from "improving the lives of our local community" to "empowering people to build strong communities globally." This evolution reflected the organization's expanded reach and diversified activities while maintaining the core focus on community empowerment.

In the corporate sector, a well-known example involves a major fast-food chain transitioning to emphasize healthier options alongside its traditional offerings. The company's original purpose of "serving quick, affordable meals" evolved to "offering balanced meal choices to enrich life's journey." This redefined purpose allowed the company to align itself with changing consumer preferences and public health narratives.

Key lessons learned from these examples include:

- Be open to change but stay true to your core values. An evolved purpose should represent both where the organization is headed and where it has been.

- Include stakeholders in the reevaluation process. Feedback from team members, customers, and other key stakeholders can provide invaluable insights into what your new purpose statement should encompass.

- Assess the current landscape, both internal and external. Purpose should be aligned with present realities as well as future ambitions. Understanding current market conditions, societal values, and internal capabilities is crucial for this.

- Effective communication is key. Once a new purpose has been defined, it's essential to communicate it clearly and consistently across all channels to ensure organization-wide alignment and understanding.

By examining these case studies and understanding their best practices, organizations can gain actionable insights into how to successfully navigate their own purpose evolution journey.

Common mistakes in the purpose reevaluation process can potentially derail an organization's alignment and performance. One frequent error is rushing the process. A purpose statement serves as the organization's compass; hastily revising it without adequate consideration can lead to misalignment between the organization's actions and its stated mission. Therefore, it's crucial to invest sufficient time in self-assessment, market analysis, and stakeholder input.

Another common pitfall is insufficient stakeholder engagement. When reevaluating purpose, some organizations might rely exclusively on top-level management perspectives, overlooking the input from frontline employees, customers, or other essential stakeholders. This lack of diverse insight can result in a purpose statement that is out of touch with the real challenges and opportunities the organization faces.

Neglecting to assess the external environment can also be detrimental. In the rapidly changing landscape of today's markets, societal norms, and technological capabilities, failing to account for these factors when revising a purpose statement is a missed opportunity and can even be a strategic blunder. Market trends, customer expectations, and even regulatory changes need to be taken into consideration.

Equally problematic is maintaining a status quo bias, wherein organizations stick too closely to their existing purpose statement due to fear of change or upheaval. While consistency is valuable, rigidity can hinder an organization from adapting to new realities. Your purpose statement should be flexible enough to allow for growth and change while staying true to the organization's core values.

Here are ways to avoid these common mistakes:

1. Set aside adequate time for a comprehensive reevaluation process. Include time for market research, stakeholder interviews, and internal discussions.

2. Engage a wide array of stakeholders in the process and consider employing tools like surveys or focus groups to capture diverse opinions and insights.
3. Regularly scan the external environment to understand how market conditions and societal norms might be changing, and how these changes could affect your organization's purpose.

4. Adopt a balance between consistency and flexibility.

5. Evaluate the current purpose statement critically and be willing to make substantive changes if they are warranted.

By recognizing these red flags early and taking steps to avoid common pitfalls, you can navigate the process of reevaluating your organization's purpose with greater success and less risk.

Updating your strategies and plans is a critical part of implementing a new purpose. Once you have a revised purpose statement, it's time to align it with your organization's objectives, KPIs, and operational tactics. You may need to modify ongoing projects or even launch new initiatives to ensure they align with the new direction. This alignment ensures that the day-to-day actions of the organization are in sync with its revised objectives.

Communication is the other cornerstone of effective implementation. Keeping stakeholders in the loop is crucial for gaining their support and ensuring a smooth transition. This involves more than just sending out a memo or holding a single meeting to announce the changes. Continuous, transparent dialogue about why the purpose was revised and what it means for stakeholders is essential. A multi-channel communication approach can be useful here, incorporating town hall meetings, newsletters, and even social media to reach different audiences.

Both aligning strategies and communicating with stakeholders are ongoing processes. You'll need to monitor how well your actions are aligning with the new purpose and make adjustments as necessary. Feedback from stakeholders, performance metrics, and market responses will all provide invaluable information for fine-tuning your strategies and communication efforts.

When measuring the impact of a revamped purpose, it's vital to take both a short-term and long-term view. Short-term metrics could include employee engagement scores, which could be measured through bi-weekly surveys, and customer satisfaction rates, often captured through point-of-sale questionnaires or online reviews. For example, a rise in Net Promoter Score (NPS) from 50 to 65 within three months of implementing the new purpose could indicate early success. On the financial side, you might look at quarterly revenue or profit margins.

Long-term metrics require a broader lens and a more extended timeframe. You could assess the employee retention rate over a year or the growth in customer lifetime value (CLV) over multiple years. For example, if your employee retention rate increased from 70% to 85% within a year, that could signify that the new purpose is resonating with staff.

In addition to quantitative assessments like these, qualitative assessments offer depth and nuance. You could conduct exit interviews to understand if the new purpose impacted an employee's decision to stay or leave. Customer testimonials or case studies could provide qualitative insights into how the purpose is affecting customer loyalty. For instance, comments in focus group discussions about the brand becoming more "responsible" or "aligned with my values" can be illuminating.

Another qualitative approach is sentiment analysis on social media or within customer reviews to gauge public perception. You could track the frequency and tone of words related to your purpose, such as "sustainable" or "inclusive," to see how they change over time.

In sum, a combination of short-term and long-term, as well as qualitative and quantitative metrics, offers the most comprehensive view of how successfully your new purpose has been implemented. Using real metrics, like NPS and employee retention rates, provides not only a snapshot but also an evolving picture of the new purpose's impact.

In the journey through the complexities of evolving an organizational purpose, several crucial points come to the fore. The need to reevaluate a purpose statement isn't a sign of failure, but rather an indicator of growth or change within the organization or the external environment. Whether instigated by internal shifts like leadership changes, or external forces like market dynamics or societal values, reevaluation is a strategic move aimed at alignment and relevance.

The process of reevaluation is not to be taken lightly; it demands comprehensive audits, stakeholder insights, and a deep dive into both quantitative and qualitative metrics. Tools like surveys, interviews, and real-world metrics offer invaluable data for shaping a more aligned and impactful purpose. And let's not forget the often-underestimated value of team input and stakeholder involvement for a collective buy-in, which can make or break the successful implementation of a new purpose.

As you move forward, the next crucial stage is ongoing monitoring and future planning. Metrics should continue to be scrutinized and strategies should be adapted as needed, ensuring that the new purpose is not just a statement on a wall but a living, breathing guide for organizational behavior. Keep an eye out for red flags and pitfalls that may indicate the need for further tweaks or even another major reevaluation.

To help you sustain this ongoing effort, the forthcoming chapters will delve into how to maintain the momentum of a purpose-driven organization, ensuring that your purpose remains a true north, guiding not just strategic decisions but also daily activities across all levels.

Exercise 11: Reevaluating Your Organization's Purpose – A Workshop

Objective: To engage your team in the reevaluation of your organization's purpose statement and to gather diverse perspectives that could inform an updated version.

Duration:
2-3 hours

Materials Needed:

Whiteboards or flip charts
Markers
Sticky notes
Laptops or tablets for research

Instructions:

Pre-Workshop Preparation:
Ask team members to review the current purpose statement and any relevant organizational materials.

Introduction (15 minutes):
Briefly outline the reason for reevaluating the organization's purpose. Discuss the agenda for the workshop.

Audit the Existing Purpose (20 minutes):
Break into small groups and ask each to list the strengths and weaknesses of the existing purpose statement. Share findings with the larger group and note common themes.

Internal and External Factors (30 minutes):
Divide into two groups. One will focus on internal factors like leadership changes that might necessitate a new purpose; the other

will discuss external factors such as market changes. Each group should present their findings and lead a brief discussion.

Stakeholder Insights (20 minutes):
Discuss who the organization's primary stakeholders are and what their likely views on the purpose might be. Capture these insights for later analysis.

Drafting a New Purpose (40 minutes):
Based on discussions, ask each small group to draft a revised purpose statement. Share these drafts and note common elements or themes.

Action Steps (20 minutes):
Discuss the steps for formally adopting this new purpose, such as incorporating it into strategy documents or communicating it to the larger organization.

Wrap-Up (10 minutes):

Summarize key insights from the workshop and outline the next steps in the reevaluation process. Collect all the drafts, insights, and discussion points for a more thorough analysis after the workshop. This will help in crafting a revised purpose statement that has wide buy-in and is better aligned with both internal and external realities.

Part V: Case Studies and Conclusion

Part V serves as the culminating segment of this book, bringing together a rich tapestry of expert opinions, real-world case studies, and synthesized insights. The aim is to not just summarize what has been discussed, but to also provide practical applications and perspectives from leaders who have successfully implemented purpose-driven initiatives in their organizations.

Chapter 12 delves deep into case examples from purpose-driven leaders. These aren't merely anecdotes; they are structured insights and advice drawn from the experiences of people who have successfully navigated the complexities associated with leading with purpose. Whether you're an entrepreneur leading a startup or a CEO steering a multinational corporation, the stories and learnings from these leaders provide a valuable roadmap for how purpose can be effectively harnessed.

Following the case studies, the Conclusion will encapsulate the key takeaways from the book. This section isn't merely a recap but will also serve as a final call to action. Here, we will draw connections between the theoretical and practical elements discussed in earlier chapters to help you integrate these learnings into your leadership style effectively.

Finally, the Appendices offer an assortment of tools and resources to help you on your journey towards becoming a purpose-driven leader. From suggested readings to concrete resources for implementing strategies discussed in this book, the appendices are designed to be a go-to guide for your continued learning.

As we enter this final part, we hope that the lessons, stories, and resources provided can serve as both inspiration and practical guide as you navigate the complexities and rewards of purpose-driven leadership.

Chapter 12: Case Examples from Purpose-Driven Leaders

Studying real-life examples holds immeasurable value in the realm of leadership development, especially for understanding the nuances of leading with purpose. These concrete cases not only offer actionable insights but also allow for an in-depth exploration of how various strategies can play out in different contexts. The lessons are far more vivid when they're grounded in actual experiences rather than abstract principles alone.

In this chapter, you'll be introduced to a collection of influential leaders, each hailing from diverse backgrounds and sectors. We will look at the effectiveness of purpose-driven leadership through the lenses of government, technology, environmental activism, entrepreneurship, organizational development, sports, and the creative arts. The individuals featured—Jacinda Ardern, Tim Cook, Greta Thunberg, Hamdi Ulukaya, Satya Nadella, Serena Williams, Kumail Nanjiani, and Emily V. Gordon—exemplify purposeful leadership in their own unique ways. They demonstrate that the principles of leading with purpose can be applied universally, no matter the scale or field in which you operate.

By delving into their stories, we hope to illuminate the essential components of leading with a defined sense of purpose, offering you practical tools and strategies that you can adapt to fit your own leadership style and objectives.

Jacinda Ardern, Prime Minister of New Zealand, has become a global symbol of compassionate governance, particularly highlighted by her country's response to the COVID-19 pandemic. While the rest of the world grappled with rapidly rising infection rates and overloaded healthcare systems, New Zealand quickly implemented stringent measures that succeeded in minimizing the spread of the virus. What sets Ardern apart isn't just effective policymaking but her underlying philosophy of leadership—leading with empathy and compassion.

The New Zealand government's response to COVID-19 was fundamentally rooted in concern for the well-being of its citizens. Ardern didn't just issue mandates; she explained them in clear, understandable language and regularly updated the public on the government's actions and thinking. She spoke not just as a leader but also as a fellow citizen, understanding and acknowledging the collective sacrifices made. This human touch turned governmental directives into collective action, fostering a national spirit of unity and cooperation.

What can governmental leaders learn from Ardern's approach? First, the power of empathy should never be underestimated. Ardern shows that empathy does not weaken leadership; it strengthens it. Being able to put oneself in another's shoes is essential for effective governance, especially during crises.

Second, transparent communication is key. Leaders should not only be clear about what is being done but also why it is being done. This fosters trust and helps citizens understand the rationale behind difficult decisions, making them more likely to comply.

Lastly, it's essential to recognize that leading with purpose means putting the welfare of the governed at the forefront. Ardern's actions reflect a deeply held belief that leadership is not just about holding power but about wielding it responsibly, guided by the principle of collective well-being. This serves as an inspiring model for any leader seeking to serve with purpose and integrity.

Tim Cook took over as CEO of Apple in 2011, succeeding the iconic Steve Jobs. While Cook had enormous shoes to fill, he carved out his unique leadership style, rooted in ethical values, particularly regarding privacy and sustainability. Apple under

Cook has become a standard-bearer in both these arenas, setting an example for other corporations to follow.

Privacy has been one of the cornerstones of Cook's leadership at Apple. In a world where data breaches and personal information misuse are increasingly common, Cook has been adamant about making Apple devices secure and private. The company has implemented stringent privacy protocols and has even taken on governmental agencies, as in the San Bernardino case, to protect customer data. Cook's stance on privacy goes beyond just technology; it's about upholding the principle that individual freedom and dignity are paramount. Apple's commitment to privacy has not only earned it the trust of its users but has also set a high standard for the tech industry, pushing other companies to enhance their privacy measures.

On the sustainability front, Cook has been equally transformative. Apple has ambitious goals to become carbon neutral across its entire business, manufacturing supply chain, and product life cycle by 2030. Under Cook's leadership, Apple has made significant investments in renewable energy and has also taken steps to reduce its environmental footprint, from the materials used in products to the packaging. Cook views sustainability not as a trade-off but as an integral part of doing good business. He has been clear that for Apple, doing what is right for the planet is also smart economics.

Cook's ethical leadership offers invaluable lessons for corporate leaders. Firstly, aligning a company's strategies with ethical principles is not just good PR—it's good business. Privacy and sustainability are not peripheral to Apple's operations; they are integrated into its core functions and even serve as selling points for its products. Secondly, purpose-driven leadership requires action, not just words. Cook doesn't just talk about privacy and sustainability; he has institutionalized these values in Apple's policies and practices. Lastly, ethical leadership fosters trust and brand loyalty, which are indispensable assets in today's competitive business landscape. Tim Cook's leadership at Apple illustrates how commitment to ethical values can shape a corporation's policies, build trust, and ultimately drive long-term success.

Greta Thunberg's impact on the global conversation about climate change is nothing short of extraordinary. Starting as a lone 15-year-old student sitting outside the Swedish Parliament with a sign reading "Skolstrejk för klimatet" (School strike for climate), she ignited a global youth movement for climate action that has mobilized millions. Greta's journey serves as a seminal case for understanding the power of purpose-driven leadership, especially among young emerging leaders.

Greta's call to action wasn't rooted in political power or financial backing; it was rooted in a genuine concern for the planet and a strong sense of purpose. Her Fridays for Future movement gained rapid momentum, thanks to her clarity of mission and the raw, emotional intensity with which she spoke. Greta's speeches at the United Nations and other global platforms were both a scathing critique of political inaction and a rallying cry for urgent change. She has managed to do what many seasoned politicians and activists could not—place climate change at the forefront of global discourse.

One of the key lessons emerging leaders can learn from Greta Thunberg is the importance of authenticity. Greta's influence was magnified because people around the world recognized her genuine concern for the climate crisis. She didn't have a hidden agenda; she was a young person worried about her future, and that resonated with millions of others around the globe. Another takeaway is the power of simplicity in communication. Greta's messages are straightforward, direct, and devoid of jargon, making them accessible and impactful.

Another crucial lesson is the role of resilience and tenacity. Greta faced considerable backlash from political leaders, media outlets, and online trolls. However, she remained steadfast in her mission, demonstrating that purpose-driven leadership often entails standing firmly against adversity.

Lastly, Greta's story emphasizes that you don't need formal authority to lead. Leadership can come from anywhere and anyone, regardless of age or position. What you need is a clear purpose, the courage to act on it, and the ability to inspire others to join you. Greta Thunberg's global impact underscores the profound influence an individual can have when fueled by a compelling purpose, offering a valuable case study for emerging leaders in any field.

Hamdi Ulukaya, the founder and CEO of Chobani, has disrupted the dairy industry not just with his company's yogurt but also through his revolutionary approach to business leadership. One of Ulukaya's most notable initiatives has been giving his employees a stake in the company. In 2016, he granted Chobani employees shares worth up to 10% of the company's value, effectively turning many of them into millionaires overnight. This wasn't a publicity stunt; it was an extension of Ulukaya's belief that employees should share in the fruits of their labor and be treated as true partners in the business.

Ulukaya's philosophy extends beyond equity shares; he also provides generous employee benefits, including above-average wages, comprehensive healthcare plans, and paid parental leave. These benefits have produced tangible results for the company, including lower turnover rates and higher employee engagement, both of which have a positive impact on productivity and the company's bottom line.

For entrepreneurs and small business leaders, Ulukaya's approach serves as a compelling model. It demonstrates the benefits of investing in your workforce, not just as a line item on a budget sheet but as valuable stakeholders in the company's success. By taking this approach, Ulukaya has created a culture of loyalty, respect, and shared responsibility, which has propelled Chobani to its position as a leader in the dairy industry.

Ulukaya's employee-first approach also points to a broader trend in the business world: the shift toward socially responsible and ethical leadership. It serves as a concrete example that doing good for your employees and doing well in business are not mutually exclusive; in fact, they often go hand in hand.

The impact of this leadership style is twofold. First, it challenges the traditional hierarchy of business and opens up the possibility for more inclusive and equitable corporate cultures. Second, it provides a blueprint for how companies can be both profitable and ethical, resonating with a consumer base that increasingly values social responsibility.

Hamdi Ulukaya's leadership at Chobani offers critical lessons for today's entrepreneurs and small business leaders. He has shown that putting employees first is not just morally right but also a smart business decision. His actions have not only benefitted his workforce but have also had a positive impact on his company's performance, providing a valuable example of how purpose-driven leadership can shape the future of business.

Satya Nadella took the helm of Microsoft in 2014, at a time when the tech giant seemed to have lost its edge, lagging behind competitors like Apple and Google. However, under Nadella's leadership, Microsoft underwent a significant transformation, not just in terms of its products and services but, perhaps more crucially, in its organizational culture. One of Nadella's early moves was to shift the company's culture towards one of greater inclusivity and openness. He introduced a growth mindset philosophy, encouraging employees to learn from failure, and to collaborate rather than operate in silos.

Nadella understood that technological innovation couldn't be the sole driving force behind Microsoft's revival; the change needed to start from within. To help accomplish this, he made diversity and inclusion a priority. For instance, Microsoft has invested in programs designed to attract a more diverse range of talent and has introduced initiatives aimed at making its workplace more inclusive for people with disabilities. Under his leadership, the company has also been more transparent about its diversity statistics, even when they reflect poorly on the company, signaling a commitment to real change rather than just lip service.

But it's not just about diversity in terms of ethnicity or gender; Nadella's inclusivity push also aimed at creating an environment where different ideas and approaches are welcomed, not shunned. This fundamental shift has had a ripple effect on Microsoft's products and services, making them more adaptable and responsive to consumer needs. As a result, the company has seen a resurgence in its growth, re-establishing itself as a leader in the tech industry.

For leaders tasked with organizational change, Nadella's tenure at Microsoft provides a plethora of takeaways. First, he shows that culture change is a long-term investment but one that is necessary for sustainable growth. Second, Nadella demonstrates the importance of leading by example. His openness about learning and growing has set the tone for the rest of the organization. Finally, the Microsoft story under Nadella's leadership underscores that when a company takes steps to be more inclusive, the benefits extend beyond the employees to positively impact the organization's products, services, and overall success.

Nadella's revitalization of Microsoft proves that organizational culture is far more than a buzzword; it's a critical business asset that can drive transformative change. His focus on inclusivity and openness has not only turned Microsoft around but has also made it a case study in how purpose-driven leadership can effectively alter the course of a large, established organization for the better.

Serena Williams is not just a record-breaking tennis player; she's also a savvy entrepreneur, philanthropist, and venture capitalist. While her athletic prowess has been the centerpiece of her public image, her skills in business and leadership deserve equal attention. Serena Williams exemplifies what it means to excel in multiple fields, leveraging her fame, capital, and influence to create opportunities for others, especially for underrepresented groups in business.

Williams has shown resilience, discipline, and an unparalleled level of competitiveness. She has displayed excellent leadership qualities on and off the court, mentoring younger athletes, and always pushing the envelope of what is achievable in tennis. Her ability to come back stronger after setbacks—be it injuries, controversies, or personal challenges—makes her an example for not just athletes but leaders in any field.

What's remarkable about Williams is her seamless transition into the world of entrepreneurship. She has invested in various sectors from fashion and beauty to tech, with a focus on companies founded by women and minorities. She launched her own fashion line, 'Serena', and has invested in more than 50 startups through her venture firm, Serena Ventures. Unlike many celebrities who lend their name to businesses, Williams is hands-on, carefully vetting the companies she gets involved with and playing an active role in their development.

Her approach to entrepreneurship shows an extension of the qualities she embodies in sports: resilience, vision, and an eagerness to break new ground. It serves as a powerful example for athletes or anyone in specialized fields looking to diversify their careers. Diversifying isn't just about risk mitigation; it's also about leveraging one's unique skills and perspectives to create value in different arenas.

So, what can aspiring leaders or those at the crossroads of sports and business learn from Serena Williams? First, excellence in one field does not preclude success in another. It is possible to transfer skills such as discipline, strategic thinking, and resilience into completely different domains. Second, diversification can lead to not just financial gain but also a more significant societal impact. Through her venture firm, Williams amplifies voices and initiatives that might otherwise go unheard or unfunded. Lastly, leadership transcends the boundaries of any single profession. A true leader inspires, breaks barriers, and creates opportunities, no matter the arena.

Serena Williams offers a masterclass in how an individual can excel in multiple areas while staying true to their core values and leveraging their success for a greater good. She embodies the versatility, impact, and depth of what purpose-driven leadership can achieve.

Kumail Nanjiani and Emily V. Gordon turned a personal crisis into a creative tour de force with their critically acclaimed film "The Big Sick." The duo, who are married in real life, co-wrote the screenplay based on their own life experiences, especially focusing on a severe illness that Emily faced, which landed her in a coma. What could have remained a private ordeal became the inspiration for a film that was not only commercially successful but also served as a platform to discuss rarely depicted cultural nuances and healthcare challenges.

The journey from real-life crisis to cinematic storytelling was no easy feat and required a high level of creative collaboration between Nanjiani and Gordon. Here, purpose served as a guiding light. The film was not merely a dramatized retelling of their story, but an endeavor to bring to the fore issues that they deeply cared about—cross-cultural relationships, the immigrant experience in America, and the emotional and financial toll of healthcare.

As both partners came from different professional backgrounds—Nanjiani a comedian and actor, Gordon a writer and therapist—they had to find a way to meld their unique skill sets effectively. The result was a script that was deeply personal, culturally insightful, and universally relatable. Nanjiani brought his comedic timing and understanding of performance to the table, while Gordon contributed her writing prowess and psychological insights.

The film's success showed that authentic, purpose-driven creative projects could resonate widely, affecting both social discourse and box-office numbers. It garnered nominations for major awards and achieved critical and commercial acclaim, but perhaps more importantly, it triggered conversations around the subjects it touched on.

What lessons does this offer to those in creative fields? For starters, the concept of 'write what you know' can transcend cliché when it's fueled by a genuine purpose. Second, collaboration is most effective when each party brings a unique perspective and skill set to the project, but this requires open communication and compromise. Finally, authenticity resonates. In an age where audiences are inundated with content, sincerity stands out. Authentic stories that come from a real place and tackle genuine issues have the potential to break through the noise.

Nanjiani and Gordon's experience illustrates how a purpose-driven approach to creativity can yield not only a commercially successful product but also one that has a significant societal impact. Their collaborative effort shines as an example for anyone looking to marry personal experience, professional skill, and larger societal themes into a coherent, impactful narrative.

The case studies of Jacinda Ardern, Tim Cook, Greta Thunberg, Hamdi Ulukaya, Satya Nadella, Serena Williams, and Kumail Nanjiani and Emily V. Gordon reveal that purpose-driven leadership can manifest in various fields, from politics and technology to activism, sports, and the arts. Despite their different domains, several recurring principles and tactics stand out among these leaders.

Firstly, empathy and compassion are common threads. Jacinda Ardern's handling of the COVID-19 crisis was steeped in compassion, while Tim Cook's commitment to privacy and sustainability reflects a concern for both users and the environment. Even in the world of business, Hamdi Ulukaya's employee-first approach at Chobani shows a level of care for his staff that goes beyond the bottom line.

Secondly, these leaders are all highly adaptive and demonstrate a willingness to change in response to new information or circumstances. Whether it's Satya Nadella shifting Microsoft's corporate culture or Serena Williams venturing into entrepreneurship, adaptability is key. Greta Thunberg began her activism as a solitary climate striker and adapted to become the face of a global movement, indicative of her ability to adjust and escalate her methods to achieve her purpose.

Thirdly, a theme of inclusivity runs through many of these leaders' stories. Nadella's focus on inclusivity rejuvenated Microsoft's internal culture. Similarly, the film "The Big Sick" told a story that broke cultural barriers, showing that creative collaboration could bring underrepresented narratives into mainstream discourse. Serena Williams has used her platform to speak against gender inequality and racial injustice, extending her influence beyond the tennis court.

They all understand the power of communication in achieving their goals. Whether it's Ardern's clear and consistent COVID-19 briefings or Thunberg's impactful speeches, effective communication is crucial. Tim Cook has made Apple's stand on ethical issues clear through open letters and public speeches. Similarly, Serena Williams and Hamdi Ulukaya use their platforms to openly discuss broader issues they care about, thereby aligning their personal brand with their purpose.

These principles align closely with the core tenets of purpose-driven leadership discussed earlier in this book—empathy, adaptability, inclusivity, and effective communication. These case studies serve not just as inspiring stories but also as practical examples that demonstrate how these principles can be applied successfully in various contexts. They reinforce the notion that purpose-driven leadership is not restricted to one particular sector but is a universally applicable approach that can drive success and create impact.

Exercise 12: Discover Your Own Case Study Through Mentor Interview

Objective: To enable students to deepen their understanding of purpose-driven leadership by conducting an interview with a mentor or leader they admire. This exercise aims to identify real-world examples and gather insights that resonate on a personal level.

Materials Needed:

Recording device (optional)
Notebook and pen
Instructions:

1. Identify a Mentor: Choose a mentor or leader you admire. This could be a professor, a manager at your workplace, a community leader, or even a family member who has demonstrated exceptional leadership qualities.
2. Reach Out: Contact your chosen mentor and request a 30-60 minute interview. Explain the purpose and what you hope to gain from the interaction.
3. Prepare Questions: Create a list of 8-10 questions aimed at uncovering the principles, challenges, and tactics related to purpose-driven leadership. For instance:
- How do you define your purpose as a leader?
- Can you share an example of a difficult decision you made that was guided by your purpose?
- What are some strategies you use to instill a sense of purpose in your team?
4. Conduct the Interview: Arrange and conduct the interview. Be respectful of their time, and make sure to either record the conversation (with permission) or take diligent notes.

5. Analyze and Report: After the interview, review your notes or recording. Identify key takeaways, common themes, and any surprising insights.
6. Share with the Class: Prepare a short presentation or write-up summarizing what you learned from the interview. Focus on how your mentor's experiences and insights can be generalized to broader principles of purpose-driven leadership.

After completing the exercise, consider sending a thank-you note to your mentor, perhaps sharing some of the insights you gained from the interview. This not only shows appreciation but also helps maintain a positive relationship for future interactions.

By the end of this exercise, you should have a richer, more nuanced understanding of what purpose-driven leadership looks like in practice.

Conclusion

As we come to the end of this journey exploring purpose-driven leadership, it's essential to pause and reflect on the ground we've covered. From understanding the foundational elements of purposeful leadership to diving deep into case studies that illuminate these principles in action, we have tackled a comprehensive range of topics. This conclusion serves as both a synthesis of these key points and a guide for implementing them in your own leadership approach. Let's revisit some of these critical areas before we conclude.

In this book, we began by delving into the core concepts of purpose and motivation, laying the groundwork for understanding why they are vital in today's leadership landscape. We explored various leadership styles that inspire, including transformational and servant leadership, and discussed strategies for building a culture of inspiration within teams.

Moving on, we tackled the challenges and obstacles that can arise, particularly during crises, and offered pragmatic strategies for overcoming them. We then shifted focus to the crucial task of measuring your impact, utilizing both quantitative and qualitative metrics to assess performance, team morale, and societal impact. Understanding that purpose is not static, we also examined the evolving nature of purpose statements and provided a roadmap for when and how to reevaluate them.

We enriched our understanding through real-world case studies, learning from leaders who have effectively employed purpose-driven strategies in diverse sectors—from politics and technology to sports and entertainment.

All of these elements come together to paint a holistic picture of purpose-driven leadership, demonstrating its versatile power across different situations and sectors.

The insights garnered from real-world case studies offer a level of practical wisdom that theoretical discussions often lack. While theories and models create the conceptual framework for understanding purpose-driven leadership, the case studies make these concepts tangible. They show us how the principles play out in real-life scenarios, with all the complexities and nuances that come with it.

These real-world examples serve as both inspiration and cautionary tales. They allow us to see the results of applying purpose-driven principles in diverse contexts, from governmental decisions affecting millions to startup cultures impacting a small team of employees. Observing how experienced leaders navigate challenges, evolve, and measure impact provides us with actionable blueprints that can be customized for our own unique situations.

Studying these cases helps to reinforce the adaptability and efficacy of purpose-driven leadership across industries. Whether you are in technology, healthcare, politics, or the arts, the basic tenets of leading with purpose remain the same. It's about understanding your core values, articulating a clear vision, and mobilizing your team or community towards achieving common goals. The case studies serve as compelling evidence that these principles have universal applicability and can drive success in any field.

As we move to the conclusion, remember that these real-world insights are not just interesting anecdotes; they are essential tools for your leadership toolkit. They bring theoretical discussions into focus and provide a pragmatic approach to adopting purpose-driven leadership in your own life. They make the abstract concrete, showing you not just why you should lead with purpose, but how.

The versatility of purpose-driven leadership is one of its most remarkable attributes. Unlike management models that are geared toward specific industries or types of organizations, the principles of leading with a strong sense of purpose are universally applicable. From the nonprofit sector aiming for social change to for-profit corporations targeting market dominance, the core tenets hold true: a clear purpose fosters unity, drives innovation, and leads to sustainable success.

Take, for example, the healthcare sector. Here, purpose-driven leadership could mean rallying your team around the goal of providing compassionate, high-quality care. This singular focus can improve patient outcomes, enhance staff satisfaction, and even streamline operations.

In the tech industry, where rapid innovation is the name of the game, a well-defined purpose can serve as a lighthouse, helping to navigate the stormy seas of market competition and technological obsolescence. For instance, a purpose rooted in making technology accessible to all could guide product development, customer engagement, and even internal hiring practices.

In creative fields such as film, art, or writing, purpose-driven leadership can manifest in deeply personal ways. The focus might be on telling stories that need to be heard or bringing underrepresented perspectives into the spotlight. This sense of purpose not only fuels the creative process but can also impact how work is received and who it reaches.

Even in sports, where physical prowess is often the primary focus, purpose-driven leadership has a role to play. Coaches who instill a sense of shared purpose, whether it's about achieving personal bests or working as a cohesive unit, can significantly boost team morale and performance.

The versatility of purpose-driven leadership is evident not just across fields but also in scenarios ranging from crisis management to long-term strategic planning. Whether you're navigating a company through a difficult market transition or spearheading a community initiative that will take years to come to fruition, a clearly defined purpose offers both the compass and the roadmap.

As we wrap up our discussions, remember that purpose-driven leadership is not a one-size-fits-all model. It's a flexible approach that adapts to different needs, goals, and contexts. This versatility is what makes it not just a management trend but a timeless principle that can guide you through the multiple, diverse challenges and opportunities that leadership inevitably entails.

In concluding this exploration of purpose-driven leadership, the overarching message can be distilled into a simple yet profound truth: leading with a clear, well-articulated purpose is not merely a strategy for success—it is a fundamental principle that has the power to transform individuals, teams, and entire organizations. This transformation is not just about hitting milestones or boosting bottom lines; it's about creating work environments that inspire, decision-making processes that empower, and business models that have a far-reaching positive impact.

Purpose-driven leadership is not a fleeting trend or a catchphrase; it's an enduring approach grounded in the understanding that meaningful change and sustainable growth are only achievable when there is a foundational sense of purpose guiding the way. It goes beyond quarterly earnings and performance evaluations, making its presence felt in how a company responds to crises, how it evolves, and how it measures and interprets its own impact.

We illustrated the concepts by a diverse range of case studies and showed that purpose-driven leadership is universally relevant. It's not confined to a particular industry, nor is it exclusive to CEOs and executives. Whether you're an emerging leader or a seasoned veteran, in healthcare or in tech, working for a small startup or a multinational corporation, the principles of purpose-driven leadership can enrich your professional journey.

Before you turn the final page of this book, consider it not the end but a beginning. A beginning to a more conscious, fulfilling, and effective way of leading. The theories, strategies, and real-world examples shared here are tools for you to wield, but the most potent tool you have is your ability to lead with purpose. This is the lens through which complexities become clear, challenges become surmountable, and true leadership is realized. Keep this principle at the forefront of your leadership approach, and you'll not only find professional success but also attain a deeper sense of personal fulfillment and make a meaningful impact on the world around you.

As you move forward in your leadership journey, don't just consider the principles of purpose-driven leadership as something you've learned—think of them as a call to action. The insights, strategies, and examples we've explored are meant to be applied, tested, and refined in the real world. This is your chance to make a significant, lasting impact not just in your organization, but in your own life and in the communities that you serve.

It's easy to read about purpose and agree with its importance, but the real transformation happens when you actively integrate these principles into your daily decision-making and long-term strategies. Start with small, actionable steps: revisit your own sense of purpose or the purpose of your team or organization. Open up a dialogue with your colleagues, engage in meaningful conversations, and be open to change and adaptation. Look for ways to measure your impact, not just through profits or productivity, but through the more nuanced metrics of employee well-being, customer satisfaction, and community impact.

Remember, purpose-driven leadership is not a solo endeavor. Invite others to participate in this journey with you. Collaborate, support, and most importantly, lead by example. Show that it's not just about what you achieve, but how you achieve it—that purpose and performance are not mutually exclusive but are, in fact, mutually reinforcing.

Don't wait for the perfect moment; the time to act is now. The journey to becoming a purpose-driven leader is both a personal and collective responsibility, and it's one that promises rewards far greater than conventional measures of success. Take the first step today and let the power of purpose guide you towards a more meaningful, impactful future.

Appendices

Tools and Resources for Purpose-Driven Leadership

In the realm of purpose-driven leadership, having the right tools and resources can make a significant difference. From understanding your core motivations to improving team dynamics and personal well-being, there are a variety of resources that can guide you on this journey.

- "Start With Why" TED Talk by Simon Sinek: Offers foundational insights into the importance of understanding your "why" in leadership.

- StrengthsFinder 2.0 by Tom Rath: An assessment tool that identifies individual strengths for better team dynamics and personal growth.

- "Leadership and Self-Deception" by The Arbinger Institute: Focuses on psychological barriers in leadership and strategies for overcoming them.

- Harvard Business Review Articles: A collection of studies and insights on various aspects of purpose-driven leadership.

- Mindfulness Apps (Headspace, Calm): Useful for stress management and improving focus and decision-making in leadership contexts.

- Emotional Intelligence 2.0 by Travis Bradberry & Jean Greaves: This book includes a test for measuring your emotional intelligence, a crucial skill in leadership.

- Project Management Tools (Asana, Trello): These platforms help in efficient task management, allowing leaders to focus on the bigger picture.

- "Dare to Lead" by Brené Brown: Explores the role of vulnerability and courage in leadership.

- Coursera Leadership Courses: Online courses from accredited universities on various leadership topics.

- Slack for Team Communication: An essential tool for modern leadership, promoting transparency and open communication.

- "Good to Great" by Jim Collins: Examines why some companies make the leap to greatness and others don't, valuable for leaders aiming for long-term success.

- G Suite: Offers a range of productivity and collaboration tools helpful for remote or in-person teams.

- Evernote for Notetaking: Keeps your ideas, minutes of meetings, and important information well-organized.

- "The Lean Startup" by Eric Ries: Focuses on a new approach to business that's being adopted around the world.

- LinkedIn Learning: Offers a plethora of courses on leadership skills from negotiation to conflict resolution.

Reading Materials for Purpose Driven Leadership

- "The Five Dysfunctions of a Team" by Patrick Lencioni: Explores common challenges teams face and how to overcome them.

- "Quiet: The Power of Introverts in a World That Can't Stop Talking" by Susan Cain: A look at how introverts can also be effective leaders.

- "The Art of Happiness" by Dalai Lama: Focuses on the importance of empathy and compassion in leadership.

- "The Innovator's Dilemma" by Clayton Christensen: Discusses how companies can do everything "right" and still lose market leadership.

- "Man's Search for Meaning" by Viktor Frankl: Offers profound insights on purpose and the importance of attributing meaning to work and life.

- "Radical Candor" by Kim Scott: A guide on how to be a kick-ass boss without losing your humanity.

- "Seven Habits of Highly Effective People" by Stephen Covey: Provides a principle-centered approach for solving personal and professional problems.

- "How to Win Friends and Influence People" by Dale Carnegie: A classic that offers basic techniques in handling people and how to have people like you.

- "Leading Change" by John Kotter: Discusses the steps to successful change and how to implement them in your organization.

- "The Servant" by James C. Hunter: A straightforward narrative on the fundamentals of servant leadership.

- "Good to Great" by Jim Collins: Explores what differentiates great companies from good ones.

- "Switch: How to Change Things When Change Is Hard" by Chip Heath and Dan Heath: Focuses on how to make effective changes.

- "Built to Last" by Jim Collins and Jerry I. Porras: Discusses the principles that lie behind enduring great companies.

- "Thinking, Fast and Slow" by Daniel Kahneman: An exploration into various modes of thought and how they affect decision-making.

- "The Lean Startup" by Eric Ries: Offers new approaches to business development and product innovation.
- "Who Moved My Cheese?" by Spencer Johnson: A motivational story that offers unique insights into dealing with change.

- "Daring Greatly" by Brené Brown: Explores the power and potential of vulnerability in leadership.

- "Mindset: The New Psychology of Success" by Carol S. Dweck: Introduces the concept of 'fixed' vs. 'growth' mindsets.

- "Leaders Eat Last" by Simon Sinek: Focuses on how leaders can create a culture that fosters trust and collaboration.

- "The Culture Code" by Daniel Coyle: Investigates the secrets of highly successful groups and how they manage to excel.

References

Introduction

Brown, Brené. "Daring Greatly: How the Courage to Be Vulnerable Transforms the Way We Live, Love, Parent, and Lead." Penguin Random House, 2012.

Coyle, Daniel. "The Culture Code: The Secrets of Highly Successful Groups." Random House, 2018.

Collins, Jim. "Good to Great: Why Some Companies Make the Leap...and Others Don't." HarperBusiness, 2001.

Collins, Jim, and Jerry I. Porras. "Built to Last: Successful Habits of Visionary Companies." HarperBusiness, 1994.

Dweck, Carol S. "Mindset: The New Psychology of Success." Random House, 2006.

Heath, Chip, and Dan Heath. "Switch: How to Change Things When Change Is Hard." Random House, 2010.

Johnson, Spencer. "Who Moved My Cheese? An Amazing Way to Deal with Change in Your Work and in Your Life." G. P. Putnam's Sons, 1998.

Kahneman, Daniel. "Thinking, Fast and Slow." Farrar, Straus and Giroux, 2011.

Ries, Eric. "The Lean Startup: How Today's Entrepreneurs Use Continuous Innovation to Create Radically Successful Businesses." Currency, 2011.

Sinek, Simon. "Leaders Eat Last: Why Some Teams Pull Together and Others Don't." Portfolio/Penguin, 2014.

Chapter 1

Avolio, Bruce J., and Bernard M. Bass. "Developing Potential Across a Full Range of Leadership: Cases on Transactional and Transformational Leadership." Psychology Press, 2002.

Blanchard, Ken, and Spencer Johnson. "The One Minute Manager." HarperCollins, 1982.

Covey, Stephen R. "The 7 Habits of Highly Effective People: Powerful Lessons in Personal Change." Simon & Schuster, 1989.

Csikszentmihalyi, Mihaly. "Flow: The Psychology of Optimal Experience." Harper & Row, 1990.

Drucker, Peter F. "The Practice of Management." Harper & Row, 1954.

Duckworth, Angela. "Grit: The Power of Passion and Perseverance." Scribner, 2016.

George, Bill. "True North: Discover Your Authentic Leadership." Jossey-Bass, 2007.

Goleman, Daniel. "Emotional Intelligence: Why It Can Matter More Than IQ." Bantam Books, 1995.

Greenleaf, Robert K. "Servant Leadership: A Journey into the Nature of Legitimate Power and Greatness." Paulist Press, 1977.

Kotter, John P. "Leading Change." Harvard Business School Press, 1996.

Lencioni, Patrick. "The Five Dysfunctions of a Team: A Leadership Fable." Jossey-Bass, 2002.

Maxwell, John C. "The 21 Irrefutable Laws of Leadership: Follow Them and People Will Follow You." Thomas Nelson, 1998.

Pink, Daniel H. "Drive: The Surprising Truth About What Motivates Us." Riverhead Books, 2009.

Sandberg, Sheryl. "Lean In: Women, Work, and the Will to Lead." Knopf, 2013.

Scharmer, Otto. "Theory U: Leading from the Future as It Emerges." Berrett-Koehler Publishers, 2009.

Yukl, Gary A. "Leadership in Organizations." Prentice-Hall, 1981.

Chapter 2

Bennis, Warren. "On Becoming a Leader." Addison-Wesley, 1989.

Brown, Brené. "Daring Greatly: How the Courage to Be Vulnerable Transforms the Way We Live, Love, Parent, and Lead." Avery, 2012.

Cameron, Kim. "Positive Leadership: Strategies for Extraordinary Performance." Berrett-Koehler, 2008.

Carnegie, Dale. "How to Win Friends and Influence People." Simon & Schuster, 1936.

Carver, John. "Boards That Make a Difference: A New Design for Leadership in Nonprofit and Public Organizations." Jossey-Bass, 1990.

Collins, Jim. "Good to Great: Why Some Companies Make the Leap... and Others Don't." Harper Business, 2001.

Collins, Jim, and Jerry I. Porras. "Built to Last: Successful Habits of Visionary Companies." HarperCollins, 1994.

Covey, Stephen M.R., and Rebecca R. Merrill. "The Speed of Trust: The One Thing That Changes Everything." Free Press, 2006.

Dweck, Carol S. "Mindset: The New Psychology of Success." Random House, 2006.

Gardner, Howard. "Frames of Mind: The Theory of Multiple Intelligences." Basic Books, 1983.

Gladwell, Malcolm. "Outliers: The Story of Success." Little, Brown and Co., 2008.

Greenleaf, Robert K. "The Power of Servant-Leadership: Essays." Berrett-Koehler Publishers, 1998.

Hackman, J. Richard, and Ruth Wageman. "A Theory of Team Coaching." Academy of Management Review, 2005.

Heifetz, Ronald A., and Martin Linsky. "Leadership on the Line: Staying Alive Through the Dangers of Leading." Harvard Business Review Press, 2002.

Kotter, John P., and Dan S. Cohen. "The Heart of Change: Real-Life Stories of How People Change Their Organizations." Harvard Business School Press, 2002.

Kouzes, James M., and Barry Z. Posner. "The Leadership Challenge: How to Make Extraordinary Things Happen in Organizations." Jossey-Bass, 2012.

Northouse, Peter G. "Leadership: Theory and Practice." Sage Publications, 1997.

Schwartz, Tony. "The Way We're Working Isn't Working." Free Press, 2010.

Senge, Peter M. "The Fifth Discipline: The Art & Practice of The Learning Organization." Doubleday, 1990.

Zenger, Jack, and Joseph Folkman. "The Extraordinary Leader: Turning Good Managers into Great Leaders." McGraw-Hill, 2002.

Chapter 3

Avolio, Bruce J., and Bernard M. Bass. "Developing Potential Across a Full Range of Leadership: Cases on Transactional and Transformational Leadership." Psychology Press, 2002.

Bandura, Albert. "Self-Efficacy: The Exercise of Control." Worth Publishers, 1997.

Block, Peter. "Stewardship: Choosing Service Over Self-Interest." Berrett-Koehler Publishers, 1993.

Brown, Brene. "Braving the Wilderness: The Quest for True Belonging and the Courage to Stand Alone." Random House, 2017.

Christensen, Clayton M., and Michael E. Raynor. "The Innovator's Solution: Creating and Sustaining Successful Growth." Harvard Business School Press, 2003.

Ciulla, Joanne B. "The Working Life: The Promise and Betrayal of Modern Work." Three Rivers Press, 2000.

Drucker, Peter F. "The Practice of Management." Harper & Row, 1954.

Fullan, Michael. "Leading in a Culture of Change." Jossey-Bass, 2001.

Goffee, Rob, and Gareth Jones. "Why Should Anyone Be Led by You? What It Takes To Be An Authentic Leader." Harvard Business Review Press, 2006.

Green, Robert L. "Practicing the Art of Leadership: A Problem-Based Approach to Implementing the ISLLC Standards." Prentice Hall, 2008.

Heath, Chip, and Dan Heath. "Made to Stick: Why Some Ideas Survive and Others Die." Random House, 2007.

Herzberg, Frederick. "One More Time: How Do You Motivate Employees?" Harvard Business Review, 1968.

Holliday, Archie. "Corporate Cultures: The Rites and Rituals of Corporate Life." Addison-Wesley, 1981.

Kaplan, Robert S., and David P. Norton. "The Balanced Scorecard: Translating Strategy into Action." Harvard Business School Press, 1996.

Kegan, Robert, and Lisa Laskow Lahey. "An Everyone Culture: Becoming a Deliberately Developmental Organization." Harvard Business Review Press, 2016.

Lencioni, Patrick. "The Five Dysfunctions of a Team: A Leadership Fable." Jossey-Bass, 2002.

Maxwell, John C. "The 21 Irrefutable Laws of Leadership: Follow Them and People Will Follow You." Thomas Nelson, 1998.

Mintzberg, Henry. "The Nature of Managerial Work." Harper & Row, 1973.

Quinn, Robert E. "Deep Change: Discovering the Leader Within." Jossey-Bass, 1996.

Wheatley, Margaret J. "Leadership and the New Science: Discovering Order in a Chaotic World." Berrett-Koehler Publishers, 1999.

Chapter 4

Amabile, Teresa M., and Steven J. Kramer. "The Progress Principle: Using Small Wins to Ignite Joy, Engagement, and Creativity at Work." Harvard Business Press, 2011.

Bass, Bernard M., and Ronald E. Riggio. "Transformational Leadership." Psychology Press, 2006.

Boyatzis, Richard E., and Annie McKee. "Resonant Leadership: Renewing Yourself and Connecting with Others Through Mindfulness, Hope, and Compassion." Harvard Business Press, 2005.

Collins, Jim. "Good to Great: Why Some Companies Make the Leap and Others Don't." HarperBusiness, 2001.

Covey, Stephen R. "The 7 Habits of Highly Effective People: Powerful Lessons in Personal Change." Simon & Schuster, 1989.

Deci, Edward L., and Richard M. Ryan. "Intrinsic Motivation and Self-Determination in Human Behavior." Plenum, 1985.

Duck, Jeanie Daniel. "The Change Monster: The Human Forces That Fuel or Foil Corporate Transformation and Change." Crown Business, 2001.

Goleman, Daniel, Richard Boyatzis, and Annie McKee. "Primal Leadership: Realizing the Power of Emotional Intelligence." Harvard Business School Press, 2002.

Hackman, J. Richard, and Greg R. Oldham. "Work Redesign." Addison-Wesley, 1980.

Kouzes, James M., and Barry Z. Posner. "The Leadership Challenge: How to Make Extraordinary Things Happen in Organizations." Jossey-Bass, 2017.

Northouse, Peter G. "Leadership: Theory and Practice." Sage Publications, 2018.

Pink, Daniel H. "Drive: The Surprising Truth About What Motivates Us." Riverhead Books, 2009.

Senge, Peter M. "The Fifth Discipline: The Art & Practice of The Learning Organization." Doubleday, 1990.

Sinek, Simon. "Leaders Eat Last: Why Some Teams Pull Together and Others Don't." Portfolio, 2014.

Tichy, Noel M., and Warren G. Bennis. "Judgment: How Winning Leaders Make Great Calls." Portfolio, 2007.

Yukl, Gary. "Leadership in Organizations." Pearson, 2012.

Chapter 5

Avolio, Bruce J., and Bernard M. Bass. "Multifactor Leadership Questionnaire." Mind Garden, 2004.

Bennis, Warren. "On Becoming a Leader." Addison-Wesley, 1989.

Blanchard, Ken, and Spencer Johnson. "The One Minute Manager." William Morrow, 1982.

Brown, Brené. "Dare to Lead: Brave Work. Tough Conversations. Whole Hearts." Random House, 2018.

Buckingham, Marcus, and Donald O. Clifton. "Now, Discover Your Strengths." Gallup Press, 2001.

Csikszentmihalyi, Mihaly. "Flow: The Psychology of Optimal Experience." Harper & Row, 1990.

Drucker, Peter F. "The Practice of Management." Harper & Row, 1954.

Edmondson, Amy C. "The Fearless Organization: Creating Psychological Safety in the Workplace for Learning, Innovation, and Growth." Wiley, 2018.

George, Bill, and Peter Sims. "True North: Discover Your Authentic Leadership." Jossey-Bass, 2007.

Greenleaf, Robert K. "Servant Leadership: A Journey into the Nature of Legitimate Power and Greatness." Paulist Press, 1977.

Heath, Chip, and Dan Heath. "Switch: How to Change Things When Change Is Hard." Broadway Books, 2010.

Herzberg, Frederick. "Work and the Nature of Man." World Publishing Company, 1966.

Kotter, John P. "Leading Change." Harvard Business School Press, 1996.

Lencioni, Patrick. "The Five Dysfunctions of a Team: A Leadership Fable." Jossey-Bass, 2002.

Maxwell, John C. "The 21 Irrefutable Laws of Leadership: Follow Them and People Will Follow You." Thomas Nelson, 1998.

McGregor, Douglas. "The Human Side of Enterprise." McGraw-Hill, 1960.

Quinn, Robert E. "Deep Change: Discovering the Leader Within." Jossey-Bass, 1996.

Rokeach, Milton. "The Nature of Human Values." Free Press, 1973.

Schein, Edgar H. "Organizational Culture and Leadership." Jossey-Bass, 2010.

Schwartz, Tony. "The Way We're Working Isn't Working: The Four Forgotten Needs That Energize Great Performance." Free Press, 2010.

Tuckman, Bruce W. "Developmental Sequence in Small Groups." Psychological Bulletin, 1965.

Vroom, Victor H., and Philip W. Yetton. "Leadership and Decision-Making." University of Pittsburgh Press, 1973.

Zenger, John, and Joseph Folkman. "The Extraordinary Leader: Turning Good Managers into Great Leaders." McGraw-Hill, 2002.

Chapter 6

Bass, Bernard M., and Ruth Bass. "The Bass Handbook of Leadership: Theory, Research, and Managerial Applications." Free Press, 2008.

Covey, Stephen R. "The 7 Habits of Highly Effective People: Powerful Lessons in Personal Change." Free Press, 1989.

Duckworth, Angela. "Grit: The Power of Passion and Perseverance." Scribner, 2016.

Dweck, Carol S. "Mindset: The New Psychology of Success." Ballantine Books, 2006.

Fiedler, Fred E. "A Theory of Leadership Effectiveness." McGraw-Hill, 1967.

Goleman, Daniel. "Emotional Intelligence: Why It Can Matter More Than IQ." Bantam Books, 1995.

Haidt, Jonathan. "The Righteous Mind: Why Good People Are Divided by Politics and Religion." Pantheon Books, 2012.

Hackman, J. Richard, and Greg R. Oldham. "Work Redesign." Addison-Wesley, 1980.

House, Robert J. "A 1976 Theory of Charismatic Leadership." In J.G. Hunt & L.L. Larson (Eds.), Leadership: The Cutting Edge, 1977.

Judge, Timothy A., and Ronald F. Piccolo. "Transformational and Transactional Leadership: A Meta-Analytic Test of Their Relative Validity." Journal of Applied Psychology, 2004.

Kahneman, Daniel. "Thinking, Fast and Slow." Farrar, Straus and Giroux, 2011.

Kouzes, James M., and Barry Z. Posner. "The Leadership Challenge: How to Make Extraordinary Things Happen in Organizations." Jossey-Bass, 2012.

Pink, Daniel H. "Drive: The Surprising Truth About What Motivates Us." Riverhead Books, 2009.

Robbins, Stephen P., and Timothy A. Judge. "Organizational Behavior." Prentice Hall, 2008.

Scharmer, Otto. "Theory U: Leading from the Future as It Emerges." Berrett-Koehler Publishers, 2007.

Seligman, Martin E.P. "Authentic Happiness: Using the New Positive Psychology to Realize Your Potential for Lasting Fulfillment." Free Press, 2002.

Chapter 7

Avolio, Bruce J., and Bernard M. Bass. "Multifactor Leadership Questionnaire." Mind Garden, 2004.

Bandura, Albert. "Self-Efficacy: The Exercise of Control." W.H. Freeman, 1997.

Blanchard, Ken, and Spencer Johnson. "The One Minute Manager." William Morrow, 1982.

Collins, Jim. "Good to Great: Why Some Companies Make the Leap and Others Don't." Harper Business, 2001.

Covey, Stephen M.R. "The Speed of Trust: The One Thing That Changes Everything." Free Press, 2006.

Csikszentmihalyi, Mihaly. "Flow: The Psychology of Optimal Experience." Harper & Row, 1990.

Deci, Edward L., and Richard M. Ryan. "Intrinsic Motivation and Self-Determination in Human Behavior." Plenum, 1985.

Drucker, Peter F. "The Effective Executive: The Definitive Guide to Getting the Right Things Done." HarperBusiness, 1967.

Gardner, Howard. "Frames of Mind: The Theory of Multiple Intelligences." Basic Books, 1983.

Gladwell, Malcolm. "Outliers: The Story of Success." Little, Brown and Company, 2008.

Greenleaf, Robert K. "Servant Leadership: A Journey into the Nature of Legitimate Power and Greatness." Paulist Press, 1977.

Heifetz, Ronald A. "Leadership Without Easy Answers." Harvard University Press, 1994.

Herzberg, Frederick. "Work and the Nature of Man." World Publishing, 1966.

Kotter, John P. "Leading Change." Harvard Business Review Press, 1996.

Lencioni, Patrick. "The Five Dysfunctions of a Team: A Leadership Fable." Jossey-Bass, 2002.

Maxwell, John C. "The 21 Irrefutable Laws of Leadership: Follow Them and People Will Follow You." Thomas Nelson, 1998.

Mintzberg, Henry. "The Nature of Managerial Work." Harper & Row, 1973.

Northouse, Peter G. "Leadership: Theory and Practice." Sage Publications, 1997.

Schein, Edgar H. "Organizational Culture and Leadership." Jossey-Bass, 1985.

Senge, Peter M. "The Fifth Discipline: The Art & Practice of the Learning Organization." Doubleday, 1990.

Sinek, Simon. "Leaders Eat Last: Why Some Teams Pull Together and Others Don't." Portfolio, 2014.

Chapter 8

Bass, Bernard M., and Ruth Bass. "The Bass Handbook of Leadership: Theory, Research, and Managerial Applications." Free Press, 2008.

Bennis, Warren. "On Becoming a Leader." Addison-Wesley, 1989.

Bolman, Lee G., and Terrence E. Deal. "Reframing Organizations: Artistry, Choice, and Leadership." Jossey-Bass, 1991.

Brown, Brené. "Daring Greatly: How the Courage to Be Vulnerable Transforms the Way We Live, Love, Parent, and Lead." Gotham, 2012.

Christensen, Clayton M. "The Innovator's Dilemma: When New Technologies Cause Great Firms to Fail." Harvard Business Review Press, 1997.

Collins, Jim, and Jerry I. Porras. "Built to Last: Successful Habits of Visionary Companies." HarperBusiness, 1994.

Covey, Stephen R. "The 7 Habits of Highly Effective People: Powerful Lessons in Personal Change." Free Press, 1989.

Csikszentmihalyi, Mihaly. "Good Business: Leadership, Flow, and the Making of Meaning." Penguin Books, 2003.

Goleman, Daniel. "Emotional Intelligence: Why It Can Matter More Than IQ." Bantam Books, 1995.

Hackman, J. Richard. "Leading Teams: Setting the Stage for Great Performances." Harvard Business Review Press, 2002.

Heath, Chip, and Dan Heath. "Switch: How to Change Things When Change Is Hard." Broadway Books, 2010.

Hill, Linda A. "Becoming a Manager: How New Managers Master the Challenges of Leadership." Harvard Business Review Press, 2003.

Kouzes, James M., and Barry Z. Posner. "The Leadership Challenge: How to Make Extraordinary Things Happen in Organizations." Jossey-Bass, 2012.

Pink, Daniel H. "Drive: The Surprising Truth About What Motivates Us." Riverhead Books, 2009.

Robbins, Stephen P. "Organizational Behavior." Pearson, 1993.

Tichy, Noel M., and Warren G. Bennis. "Judgment: How Winning Leaders Make Great Calls." Portfolio, 2007.

Wheatley, Margaret J. "Leadership and the New Science: Discovering Order in a Chaotic World." Berrett-Koehler, 1999.

Chapter 9

Argyris, Chris. "Teaching Smart People How to Learn." Harvard Business Review, 1991.

Avolio, Bruce J., and Bernard M. Bass. "Developing Potential Across a Full Range of Leadership: Cases on Transactional and Transformational Leadership." Psychology Press, 2002.

Buckingham, Marcus, and Curt Coffman. "First, Break All the Rules: What the World's Greatest Managers Do Differently." Simon & Schuster, 1999.

Collins, Jim. "Good to Great: Why Some Companies Make the Leap...and Others Don't." HarperBusiness, 2001.

Conger, Jay A., and Beth Benjamin. "Building Leaders: How Successful Companies Develop the Next Generation." Jossey-Bass, 1999.

Covey, Stephen M.R. "The Speed of Trust: The One Thing That Changes Everything." Free Press, 2006.

Drucker, Peter F. "The Effective Executive: The Definitive Guide to Getting the Right Things Done." HarperBusiness, 1967.

Friedman, Stewart D. "Total Leadership: Be a Better Leader, Have a Richer Life." Harvard Business Review Press, 2008.

Gladwell, Malcolm. "Outliers: The Story of Success." Little, Brown and Company, 2008.

Heifetz, Ronald A., and Marty Linsky. "Leadership on the Line: Staying Alive Through the Dangers of Leading." Harvard Business Review Press, 2002.

Kellerman, Barbara. "Followership: How Followers Are Creating Change and Changing Leaders." Harvard Business Press, 2008.

Kotter, John P. "Leading Change." Harvard Business Review Press, 1996.

Lencioni, Patrick. "The Five Dysfunctions of a Team: A Leadership Fable." Jossey-Bass, 2002.

Mauborgne, Renée, and W. Chan Kim. "Blue Ocean Strategy: How to Create Uncontested Market Space and Make

Competition Irrelevant." Harvard Business Review Press, 2005.

Pfeffer, Jeffrey. "Power: Why Some People Have It—and Others Don't." HarperBusiness, 2010.

Sandberg, Sheryl. "Lean In: Women, Work, and the Will to Lead." Knopf, 2013.

Senge, Peter M. "The Fifth Discipline: The Art and Practice of the Learning Organization." Currency, 1990.

Sinek, Simon. "Leaders Eat Last: Why Some Teams Pull Together and Others Don't." Portfolio, 2014.

Sutton, Robert I. "Good Boss, Bad Boss: How to Be the Best... and Learn from the Worst." Business Plus, 2010.

Chapter 10

Achor, Shawn. "The Happiness Advantage: How a Positive Brain Fuels Success in Work and Life." Currency, 2010.

Csikszentmihalyi, Mihaly. "Flow: The Psychology of Optimal Experience." Harper Perennial, 1990.

DePree, Max. "Leadership Is an Art." Dell, 1989.

Duckworth, Angela. "Grit: The Power of Passion and Perseverance." Scribner, 2016.

Edmondson, Amy C. "The Fearless Organization: Creating Psychological Safety in the Workplace for Learning, Innovation, and Growth." Wiley, 2018.

Fredrickson, Barbara L. "Positivity: Top-Notch Research Reveals the 3 to 1 Ratio That Will Change Your Life." Crown Archetype, 2009.

Grant, Adam. "Give and Take: A Revolutionary Approach to Success." Viking Press, 2013.

Goleman, Daniel. "Emotional Intelligence: Why It Can Matter More Than IQ." Bantam, 1995.

Haidt, Jonathan. "The Righteous Mind: Why Good People Are Divided by Politics and Religion." Vintage, 2012.

Kim, W. Chan, and Renée Mauborgne. "Blue Ocean Shift: Beyond Competing - Proven Steps to Inspire Confidence and Seize New Growth." Hachette Books, 2017.

Newport, Cal. "Deep Work: Rules for Focused Success in a Distracted World." Grand Central Publishing, 2016.

Pink, Daniel H. "Drive: The Surprising Truth About What Motivates Us." Riverhead Books, 2009.

Schwartz, Tony. "The Way We're Working Isn't Working: The Four Forgotten Needs That Energize Great Performance." Free Press, 2010.

Seligman, Martin E.P. "Authentic Happiness: Using the New Positive Psychology to Realize Your Potential for Lasting Fulfillment." Free Press, 2002.

Zenger, John H., and Joseph Folkman. "The Extraordinary Leader: Turning Good Managers into Great Leaders." McGraw-Hill, 2002.

Chapter 11

Ariely, Dan. "Predictably Irrational: The Hidden Forces That Shape Our Decisions." Harper, 2008.

Bock, Laszlo. "Work Rules!: Insights from Inside Google That Will Transform How You Live and Lead." Hachette, 2015.

Brown, Brené. "Dare to Lead: Brave Work. Tough Conversations. Whole Hearts." Random House, 2018.

Coyle, Daniel. "The Culture Code: The Secrets of Highly Successful Groups." Bantam, 2018.

Covey, Stephen R. "The 7 Habits of Highly Effective People." Simon & Schuster, 1989.

Duhigg, Charles. "The Power of Habit: Why We Do What We Do in Life and Business." Random House, 2012.

Ferriss, Timothy. "Tools of Titans: The Tactics, Routines, and Habits of Billionaires, Icons, and World-Class Performers." Houghton Mifflin Harcourt, 2016.

Gladwell, Malcolm. "Outliers: The Story of Success." Little, Brown and Company, 2008.

Godin, Seth. "Tribes: We Need You to Lead Us." Portfolio, 2008.

Heath, Chip, and Dan Heath. "Switch: How to Change Things When Change Is Hard." Crown, 2010.

Ibarra, Herminia. "Act Like a Leader, Think Like a Leader." Harvard Business Review Press, 2015.

Jiménez, L. David Marquet, Stephen R. Covey, and Stephen M. R. "Turn the Ship Around!: A True Story of Turning Followers into Leaders." Portfolio, 2013.

Kahneman, Daniel. "Thinking, Fast and Slow." Farrar, Straus and Giroux, 2011.

Kotter, John P. "Leading Change." Harvard Business Review Press, 1996.

Lencioni, Patrick. "The Five Dysfunctions of a Team: A Leadership Fable." Jossey-Bass, 2002.

Mauborgne, Renée, and W. Chan Kim. "Blue Ocean Strategy: How to Create Uncontested Market Space and Make the

Competition Irrelevant." Harvard Business Review Press, 2005.

Robbins, Tony. "Awaken the Giant Within: How to Take Immediate Control of Your Mental, Emotional, Physical and Financial Destiny!" Free Press, 1991.

Sandberg, Sheryl. "Lean In: Women, Work, and the Will to Lead." Knopf, 2013.

Sinek, Simon. "Leaders Eat Last: Why Some Teams Pull Together and Others Don't." Portfolio, 2014.

Sutton, Robert I. "Good Boss, Bad Boss: How to Be the Best... and Learn from the Worst." Business Plus, 2010.

Taleb, Nassim Nicholas. "Antifragile: Things That Gain from Disorder." Random House, 2012.

Thaler, Richard H., and Cass R. Sunstein. "Nudge: Improving Decisions About Health, Wealth, and Happiness." Penguin, 2008.

Chapter 12

Bass, Bernard M., and Ronald E. Riggio. "Transformational Leadership." Psychology Press, 2006.

Collins, Jim. "Good to Great: Why Some Companies Make the Leap... and Others Don't." HarperBusiness, 2001.

Edmondson, Amy C. "The Fearless Organization: Creating Psychological Safety in the Workplace for Learning, Innovation, and Growth." Wiley, 2018.

Goleman, Daniel. "Emotional Intelligence: Why It Can Matter More Than IQ." Bantam Books, 1995.

Haidt, Jonathan. "The Righteous Mind: Why Good People Are Divided by Politics and Religion." Vintage, 2012.

Kouzes, James M., and Barry Z. Posner. "The Leadership Challenge: How to Make Extraordinary Things Happen in Organizations." Wiley, 2012.

Maxwell, John C. "The 21 Irrefutable Laws of Leadership: Follow Them and People Will Follow You." HarperCollins Leadership, 1998.

Pink, Daniel H. "Drive: The Surprising Truth About What Motivates Us." Riverhead Books, 2009.